C000205236

Cal.

# Desert Midwife

*The story of Amal Boody who
having nothing yet possessing all things
followed her dream*

## Marion Osgood

LIGHTHOUSE
BOOK PUBLISHING

© Marion Osgood 2021

Lighthouse Publishing
12 Dukes Court, Bognor Road, Chichester,
PO19 8FX, United Kingdom
www.lighthousebookpublishing.com

ISBN: 978-1-910848-43-2

British Library Cataloguing in Publication Data. A catalogue record for this book is available from the British Library.

Cover by Esther Kotecha, EK Design
Layout by Lighthouse Publishing
Printed in the United Kingdom

# Table of Contents

# Commendations

As western Christians we often forget that for many centuries the Middle Eastern churches formed the heart and greatest number of the Christian church. With the decline of these churches in more recent times, it remains easy to ignore them. So it is doubly important and encouraging to read the challenging story of a Syrian Christian, whose faith and passion puts our more easy-going faith to shame. With her lovely descriptive writing Marion Osgood paints a vivid picture of Amal's bold and loving work as a midwife among the poorest and most backward desert villages of the UAE. May this book move us to pray and to witness with equal commitment and boldness! May it also be God's means of calling people to follow in Amal's footsteps in the Middle East, the heart countries of Islam!

Martin and Elizabeth Goldsmith
All Nations Christian College
UK

Pioneering medical work from a tent in a remote village on the Arabian Gulf, nurse/midwife Amal Boody had no doctors to consult with, and no electricity. Yet she managed to rescue the lives of countless mothers and newborns. This inspirational story will give you hope that for those who have the courage to take God's hand and let Him lead them – even to a desert place – anything is possible!

Deborah Meroff
Author

*Commendations*

This is a truly captivating life story of a woman whose strength of character and determination enables her to move beyond her cultural expectations to discover and follow the calling of God upon her life, and to live a life of love, selfless service and influence. Beautifully and sensitively written, this book will not fail to inspire you!

Gillian Cotterill
Commissioner
Salvation Army

Congratulations Marion; you have succeeded in describing Amal's life accurately. You brilliantly made us travel with her through all her life stages, starting from her early days in Al Kafroun, then Gaza, Lebanon, Saudi Arabia, London and Ras Al Khaimah.

Suhaila Tarazi
Director
Al Ahli Arab Hospital
Gaza City

Marion Osgood does the Christian world a service by sharing the eye-opening story of Syrian midwife Amal Boody, who earned the distinction of being the first Middle Easterner to go as a full-time Christian worker to the Gulf region. We gain rare insights on pioneering Gospel witness in the Arab world as we follow her many years of service across the Middle East, including the past fifty in an Emirati village near the Oman border - the first ten spent living and delivering babies in a tent. Her God-given spiritual and physical toughness kept her going against all odds and enabled her to draw close to women in remote desert regions by delivering their babies and sharing the Gospel with them. Be sure to put *Call the Desert Midwife* on your missionary biography "must-read list."

John Maust
President
Media Associates International

# Foreword

A few years ago, I was a guest speaker at a Christian houseparty in the hills above Beirut. The church which was hosting the houseparty was led by colleagues from Ichthus Christian Fellowship (the movement led by my husband and myself). The highlight of our first day was praying for a group of about a dozen Syrian Christians who were seeking to travel to the conference from Aleppo. There was inevitably a long hold-up for them on the border as officials checked the credentials of the group and the purpose of their excursion into Lebanon. However, eventually the border guards accepted the word of the church pastor vouching for them, and we enjoyed a weekend together of prayer, the Word, fellowship and baptisms! I have continued to pray for those Christians, who have suffered so much in their homeland, due to the war there.

So when I heard from Marion that she had met an amazing Syrian Christian woman, Amal Boody, while she was in Dubai, and had written a biography about her, my interest was quickened. Once I began reading the manuscript I was very quickly hooked! As I began reading excerpts from Amal's story to my husband, Roger, he persuaded me to read the whole book aloud to him so that he could also follow the adventures of this spiritually resourceful Syrian Christian woman, whom Marion describes so vividly.

When we finished reading Amal's life story (of her vital midwifery practice and spiritual ministry in a remote desert region of UAE) we were both silent for a moment, thinking with deep gratitude to the Lord about the key people in this account, some of them unnamed. For example, the American missionary whom Amal's father, Antonius, had found encountering unpleasant hostility when speaking about Jesus to people in a souk (market). I could not help exclaiming as I read this, that the world is sorely in need today of courageous, principled, spiritual men and women like that missionary, and Antonius and his family, who are willing to step out in faith and transform the lives of those walking in darkness and poverty.

The deeply spiritual commitment shown in Amal herself was very inspirational to us, as Roger and I thought of the Gospel flowing through the world, and the remarkable men and women of other cultures and backgrounds who have lived, or are living, lives of which 'the world is not worthy ....'

So read and receive the same inspiration! The Spirit of God will speak to you through these pages, and you will join us in giving thanks for people all over the world who will be honoured in the final day for their devotion and service to Jesus Christ.


Faith Forster
Ichthus Christian Fellowship

May 2021

# Map of the Middle East

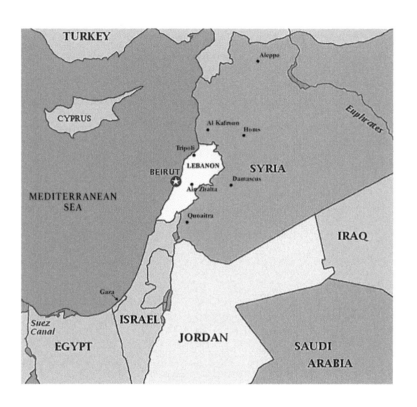

# Map of the United Arab Emirates

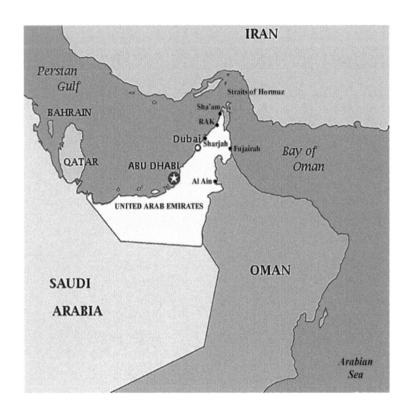

# Chapter One

## *Spring 1999*

*The doorbell rings – but I'm the only one around and it's not my house. Chopping kiwi-fruit in the kitchen while everyone else is upstairs, I try to recall what was discussed the night before. I know we're expecting Ruth, Maha... and someone called Gladys. Well I already know Ruth and Maha, so I guess it's okay for me to open the door. I prepare to greet them all enthusiastically – 'And you must be Gladys!'*

But somewhat unfairly, no-one had told me there was a change of plan. While I looked on feeling rather confused, my first ever words to Amal were causing the three on the doorstep to crease up with laughter.

I soon learnt that Amal had an enormous appetite for fun. She seemed to be the kind of person to whom funny things happened; and in her case the 'things' increased in value as they came out for repeated airings. She was indeed a gifted story-teller – but it was a God-given gift, and I soon came to realise it was used way beyond simple entertainment.

The year was 1999, and we were staying with some long-term friends in Dubai. It was Friday, their 'church' day, and we had all been preparing a buffet lunch during which my husband and I would meet some new friends – including one Amal Boody, a Syrian Christian lady. This was irresistible from the start: I had never before met anyone from Syria.

We came to the end of a kaleidoscope of a day. There had been church, then lunch, and opportunities to get to know plenty of new people. But what stood out for me was what we had begun to learn of some of the drama of Amal's unusual life. As her fun-loving exterior gave way to more thoughtful reflection, she at times held the room, recounting some of the challenges as well as the blessings of her thirty years working as a midwife in a remote desert village. For ten of those years she had lived and worked in a tent.

Already I was beginning to find her fascinating.

She talked with searing honesty; the tinge of humour seemed accidental, provoked at times by her inadvertent misuse of English idiom – until you caught the twinkle in her eye. The love and compassion she felt for the people among whom she had chosen to live in such a remote location were clearly part of her motivating force. Yet she worried too about far-away relatives for whom she felt responsible. She had chosen to turn her back on conventionality, which might have required her to stay at home and care for the ageing parents, as she was the only one unmarried among seven siblings. But perhaps for this very reason she was always concerned about family. That was only too evident to us, as she even had a younger member of her family currently under her wing, and part of the assembled company. He had found himself jobless with debts to pay – and Amal felt responsible for 'sorting him out'.

What a compelling mixture this lady was!

That evening some of us went for a walk. It was late springtime, the Dubai summer heat was already building, and it was only after dark that leaving air-conditioning behind was even thinkable. We headed to the beach where there was a hot damp breeze blowing off the sea; the atmosphere was alive with families picnicking and barbequing, children running backwards and forwards into the water, and ice-cream and drinks vendors in great demand – all in the balmy darkness. With one or two others of our party, Amal and I paddled as we walked along the shoreline, picking up lumps of coral as we went. I could not resist asking her more questions – even her background, the

Middle Eastern farming community emerging from the tail-end of the Ottoman Empire, seemed like gold dust to me.

In bits and pieces during the following few days I learnt more of her early years. Starting in her teens, and much against her parents' better judgement, she had led an adventurous life as what would now be called a charity worker, in different refugee camps in war-torn parts of the world. She had been an incurable traveller – until she discovered the cure. After qualifying as a midwife in London, she returned to the desert, finally settling in a comparatively isolated community, among the people with whom she was most happy, and where she believed her calling was; she set up on her own, with the nearest medical help being several hours' car journey away.

But the challenges which came her way did not stay hanging. Amal had a vibrant relationship with her heavenly Father – it had a down-to-earth feel to it. She talked about how she would cry out to God in the midst of disasters – and he would be there for her.

Yet the outcome wasn't always 'happily ever after'. She had at times been lonely; at times too her spiritually-tuned imagination generated irrational fears. Alone at night in her tent, she wondered what strange noises sometimes disturbed her sleep. Outcomes were often genuinely scary; occasionally they were hilarious: she certainly had the ability to tell a story against herself.

Knowing beyond a shadow of doubt that she had been 'called' to a specific life-task, she frequently wondered out loud why in spiritual terms her life was not as fruitful, particularly when it came to her Christian witness, as she had longed for it to be. When she talked like this, her vulnerability was immediate: it seemed to invite an almost parental response from the listener. She began to touch on unfulfilled longings such as I would never have identified from her usually confident and outgoing presence.

I began to feel a reverential respect for this woman, who was such a pillar of her adopted community – which was so different from her own background back in Syria. There is so much more to this woman than meets the eye, I found myself thinking.

In 2000 I was back in the same city again staying with the same friends. This time rather than with my husband I was with a travelling companion, who was well-known to my friends. I couldn't wait to introduce her to Amal.

Once again there was much coming and going, with a full timetable and plenty of celebratory spreads; a lot of it was in our honour – as guests from the home church. One evening there was an informal Bible study, and this time at the end Amal was invited to give her testimony – an opportunity for her to share at greater length how she understood she had been led by God throughout her life.

Again there was the self-effacing presentation, alongside accounts of great boldness. In her simple almost halting style she kept us all in enrapt silence for the best part of an hour. At times she made us laugh – but by the end a few were moved to tears.

So here was someone incredibly brave: deeply spiritual yet practical and resourceful, a lone traveller yet full of fun and companionship, with an almost childish sense of humour and yet at times a deep well of vulnerability. She was at home in the West, yet wedded to desert remoteness, and to losing herself in the poorest of communities.

In spite of these strong impressions, I was caught off-guard when suddenly a thought came from nowhere: why don't you write her story? This was all the more strange at the time, as up to that point I had never really written anything.

Later when Amal had left I mentioned it just as a joke: 'By the way, I'm going to write the book!'

I didn't see her for another sixteen years.

Moving forward to 2015, and our friends from Dubai were visiting us here in the UK. In the course of our time together we were out sharing a meal with them; I asked after Amal, wondering if indeed they were still in touch. 'Ah yes' one of them said; 'Amal says she is ready for you to write her story'!

By now I had had a biography published, and was much more interested in writing generally – but had long since forgotten this, my very first writing impulse. Amal might be ready, I thought – but I'm not sure I am.

At some point I must have agreed. Our friends advised an early return visit; they were planning to leave the Gulf permanently in a few months – and Amal was not getting any younger!

Meanwhile as soon as they returned home they again invited Amal to come and stay with them. They recorded a series of interviews with her, and sent me the results. Listening to them I could hear a certain amount of prompting going on; there were also frequent digressions, provoked particularly by the immediate: the smell of the next meal was clearly a major distraction. There was also a great deal of the inevitable laughter. Amal was majoring on her 'stories', the individual anecdotes of her life: the night the honey-thief came, the exploits of the faithful cockerel who guarded the tent, the privilege of being English interpreter for the Saudi royal family in the hospital in Riyadh, many years earlier... Any thought of flowing narrative, progressive chronology, or background colour and detail were obviously going to be down to me!

But there was great passion also – and stunningly clear details from her childhood: the journey on the back of a donkey to the hospital in Tripoli, when she was dying of malaria, the memory of her mother hiding her suitcase in a tree... It was as if she were gripped by the importance of what took place in those early years in her village, in her parents, and in her own life.

So in 2016 my husband and I returned to the Gulf once more. This time our friends were in Abu Dhabi.

We were excited to meet Amal again, after so many years; also on this occasion we travelled up to *Sha'am*, the remote town in the far north of the UAE which had first touched Amal with its need, all those years ago – and where she still had her home. There were signs of modernity of course, but the skinny cows still roaming the streets, the old stone houses with their palm-branch lean-to's, the barren hillsides all around – yes I recognised the back-drop to those scenes Amal recounted so vividly.

Back in Abu Dhabi and seated at our friends' coffee table Amal and I set up our interview procedure. Together, and over multiple short sittings, we gradually filled in the gaps between her stories, and pulled together the threads of her life.

Amal had never been a diary person; there were no 'papers', such as might normally be handed over to a biographer, and in fact she never gave me anything in writing at all. What I found I did have however was the memory of her voice; her distinctive accent lent a mixture of colour, genuineness and humour to the strong opinions she would often express. I could hear it on the recordings of course, but it was also in my head. I came to realise it was there at the centre of her stories, and must form a vital part of the book.

Additionally I developed links with her many friends, and a few relatives, now scattered round the world; they have helped me with details, including photos, and answered my many questions. I am extremely grateful to them all.

Here then is Amal's story.

# Chapter Two

## *In the Time of the Ottomans*

With the little girl strapped firmly to her, the woman struggled up the rough mountain path; determination overcame the heat of the day, propelling her higher, to the ancient and sacred hilltop shrine. At last she caught sight of the well, supposed source of so much more than a welcome draught of water.

The woman untied her toddler – and held her out precariously over the deep well.

---------------------

These are stony hillsides, snow-covered in winter, parched dry and scrubby in summer, sheltering peaceful valleys where rows of tall Lombardy poplars stand like sentries, and everywhere there are little walled gardens, terraced to keep the vital soil in place.

The *Al Kafroun* valley has always been like this. Here the Boody family farm sits, stone-built and timeless, against the side of the bramble-covered hill. A long walled strip of land runs from the house for half a mile or so down the valley, as far as the river below.

*This was all ours. And there was no tap in the house – just a well.*

There is a sleepy stillness in these hills, which lie between the city of Homs and the Mediterranean Sea. At 500 metres they are just high enough to attract the locals trying to escape the intense heat of the plain: here in the languid warmth of a summer afternoon, when only the buzzing of the bees can be heard, it feels as if many centuries have passed, while the valleys sleep on. From beyond the time of the biblical Patriarchs Syria has always taken its place on the Middle Eastern stage. Astride the ancient King's Highway, the only land route from Africa to Mesopotamia, whether as kingdom, caliphate, republic, or oppressed subject, Syria has always been a world-player.

Within one burnished siesta hour, it seems whole epochs have come and gone.

For the most part, Christians, Jews and Muslims lived happily side by side throughout the time of the Ottomans. But a tax was levied on Christians (unless of course they converted) by the Muslim rulers in faraway Istanbul, and sometimes this could be avoided by a strategic relocation. Amal's grandfather took his family and journeyed north from Arabia for just this purpose, settling among the Greek Orthodox communities of what is now south-west Syria. This area had always been 'Christian': a little church in every village, and round almost every bend of the mountain track, another shrine.

Amal's parents were born three years apart and in neighbouring villages, in the *Al Kafroun* Valley. Antonius Boody was the older, born in 1890. The Ottoman Empire, creaking after almost three hundred years, nevertheless had another thirty years to run.

In the days when Antonius and Hannah were growing up, children from neighbouring villages would congregate in the evenings round one of the local springs; it was the girls who fetched the water – and the boys gathered round to watch! Soon Antonius found he was watching one girl in particular – and he soon found out her name was Hannah. She even carried the cumbersome water pot more stylishly than the others. Throughout the world and still today, wherever water comes from a communal supply, it is carried by the women – and invariably on their heads. But in Antonius' eyes Hannah had taken the skill to a whole new level: using the heavy wadding of her shoulder padding as a sort of 'bung' to close the pot, she would carry the whole thing upside-down. At the same time she gave every appearance of not being in the slightest bit interested in any onlookers. She was brought up to work hard, and concentrate on the job in hand.

In fact life became harder for Hannah.

Due to increasing violence, and the disturbances marking the final years of Ottoman rule, many Syrians, Palestinians and Lebanese emigrated to South America, successfully making new lives for themselves. Hannah's father was one of these, leaving wife and children behind for a year or so, while he set himself up in Argentina. In his absence Hannah's mother spoilt her only son, Hannah's brother, and Hannah found she was doing much of the family work.

Then when she was thirteen the call came for the family to join their father. But by this time Antonius, at sixteen, was smitten. He and Hannah had become close friends – and clearly, as he saw it, with an 'understanding' in view. The possibility of now losing her was more than he could bear. He turned to the generosity of his parents: could Hannah come and live with them, to be his future bride? Convention required that the couple marry, in order for this to be possible. So the marriage was formalised; but being so young, they lived under the same roof, just not as husband and wife, for several more years. Hannah never saw her parents or brother again.

Eventually, however, the babies did start to come. Hannah and Antonius had three daughters before Amal was born. The eldest of these was Hayat, who arrived in 1920.

By this time the First World War was over, and the French mandate of Syria/Lebanon was just beginning. Deeply resented, particularly in Muslim-majority Syria, it contributed to the growth of Syrian nationalism, and the eventual drive towards an independent state of Syria. This period between the two world wars was anything but peaceful in the region; it was stormy for the Boody family also.

Three more girls followed Hayat, at intervals throughout the 1920s: Rajaa, Lydia, then finally Amal, who arrived in 1929. In those days no babies were registered. The French would have insisted on notification where they could – but birthdays were not a priority in Arab culture, and were certainly never celebrated. Amal was born in the December, and for convenience the birth was later recorded as having been on the 1st.

As the fourth girl she was not welcome. Arab traditions were strong, even within Christian communities, and one daughter was cherished – but four... Her mother's sense of shame and disappointment meant serious arguments took place between the parents, and on one occasion Hannah tossed baby Amal into her husband's lap. In later years of course her mother regretted it:

*In a dream my mother was told: 'You must love this girl as she will have many, many children.' She had asked God's forgiveness, she told my oldest sister, not long before she died.*

But in the short term there was still something she could do. A visit to the shrine on the mountain top – this would ensure the next child would be a boy. Even as she held the baby Amal out over the spring, tearfully demonstrating that she would value the birth of a boy above all else, the die was cast. She was in fact already pregnant – with a boy.

And little Amal of course was safe. In fact there were two more sons to follow; her three younger brothers were Abdullah, Raja and Robert.

# Chapter Three

## *Syria*

Amal's parents grew up at a time and in a region where it was still considered economically preferable to educate the boys rather than the girls. And having no brothers, Antonius' education would therefore be doubly important: arrangements were made and paid for by his grandmother, and at age ten he was sent to Tripoli on the coast, to attend school.

*My great-grandmother... a wise woman, respected by the village elders.*

The bustling metropolis of Tripoli was an education in itself, for this unsophisticated country boy. He had had no idea that buildings could be so grand and beautiful – or so crowded together. In the early weeks, when not in class, he wandered the streets as if in a daze; he was over-awed by the splendour of the domed and highly decorated *hammams*, Tripoli's famous Turkish baths. There were huge mosques which towered above him, confronting him for the first time with the existence of Sunni Islam. He soon realised also that there were other Christians, beside the Greek Orthodox: Armenians, Maronites, Syriacs, Roman Catholics... all had their own distinctive church buildings. Until now he had never had reason to question his family creed.

Antonius also enjoyed the labyrinthine souks, where pungent spicy aromas competed with the exotic perfumes produced by the soap-sellers. He watched spellbound as deals were struck, and rich silks and velvets changed hands as quickly as fruit and vegetables.

Then one day he discovered something novel going on: a crowd was gathering round a man who appeared to be giving out free leaflets. Trying to hide behind others, Antonius gradually shuffled closer; he wanted to hear what the man was saying to the passers-by. Suddenly someone started shouting; a stone went flying across the heads of the crowd – closely followed by another, and directed at the stranger. Antonius ducked – but still could not take his eyes off the man, who by this time had been hit.

But the man did not shout back, neither did he run away; he did not pick up a stone to throw back. Eventually most of the crowd wandered off – but Antonius was hooked. Why did this man not retaliate? Antonius plucked up courage to ask: 'Christ tells us not to' came his immediate response, his Arabic betraying a heavy American accent. Antonius was captivated by this boldness – on the part of what turned out to be a Presbyterian missionary. Lingering in the shade of the souk he thought of one question after another.

*The missionary led Antonius to Christ, and gave him a Bible. My father was a new man.*

Permanent links were forged between Antonius and his new American friend, and in the months which followed representatives from the Presbyterian mission in Tripoli came to his village back in *Al Kafroun*, and held meetings in Antonius' family home.

*In those days the whole village was Orthodox – but no house had a Bible.*

A new Christian fervour seemed to spread through the valley; many rejected the traditional aspects of religious observance with, as they saw it, the attendant superstitions. Antonius himself, while still a teenager, was fired with a new passion, launching himself out into evangelistic journeys.

As so often happens, however, not everyone was happy. In fact some, even members of the wider family, were inclined to be suspicious; they called this new 'faith' a heresy. Some villagers attacked during the house meetings, and threw stones aimed to land on the roof for maximum noise and disruption.

By this time Hannah was part of the household. Again she found herself doing much of the men's work – this time because her husband, young as he still was, was now the most highly educated man in the village. The Turkish authorities employed him to teach reading and writing, and this fitted well with his plans for roaming the valleys on horseback to preach the Gospel; he was spared the forced conscription that was the constant threat of the closing Ottoman years. His respect grew within the community; he now had a wife to look after and eventually, a growing number of children.

Hannah on the other hand never learned to read or write. She was greatly admired for many other talents however. As well as being expert at all everyday tasks she could turn her hand to some rare skills for which others seemed to need prolonged training. One day she delivered a breech baby, saving the life of both mother and baby when it was too late to reach the doctor. In her husband's frequent absences, Hannah coped with everything.

As a toddler, little Amal was captivated by her father, now a public figure in the area; not primarily a preacher, he nevertheless addressed small household groups, and distributed books and bibles from the British and Foreign Bible Society.

But in his paid role he was responsible for establishing primary education in the region, founding several village schools; thanks to him, many children, both boys and girls, were able to read and write. The schools were of a Presbyterian foundation, rather than Orthodox. Due to the French mandate, the French language had to be taught – but nobody used it: the Arabic medium was preferred, closely followed by English.

As a respected and remunerated teacher, Antonius was able to employ others to do the work on his land.

Set within the ancient Fertile Crescent, the Syrian way of life has always involved agriculture, and it was particularly a feature of this part of Syria. ('*Kafroun*' is an Aramaic word meaning 'farms'.) Antonius had vineyards which needed careful tending, and there were orchards in abundance: apples, olives, figs, pomegranates, peaches and pistachios all had to be harvested at various times, then taken to market. There were goats to keep the grass short in the orchards, a few cows to be milked, the beasts of burden to feed – and chickens getting under everyone's feet.

Some of those who worked Antonius' land would be Alawites, a minority Shi-ite Muslim group. Muslims generally did not regard the Alawi highly, considering them a sect. They would not have gone along with Alawite enthusiasm for the local Sheikh Hassan shrine, situated at the river's source, and the place where sacrifices were made. (The ruling Assad family was later to emerge from the Alawite community.)

The two communities, Christians and Alawites, worked well side-by-side, much as they had done for centuries. Their dress was not dissimilar in those days, as it later became. The older men of both groups wore the black baggy trousers of the region; the women wore headscarves (as opposed to a full head covering) – but the Alawite women's scarves and general dress were of more brightly coloured material than that of the Christians, who therefore considered them as having 'no taste'!

Soon it would be time for Amal to gain advantage from her father's educational entrepreneurship – time to start attending the school in *Mashta al-Helou*, the largest village in the valley.

When she had been a toddler her sisters had sometimes taken her with them to school. It would seem natural therefore that when it was Amal's turn, she should have to take Abdullah with her. But this was different, and proved to be a battle-ground for them both. Amal was a bright child, keen to learn, whereas at that stage Abdullah's interest and enthusiasm had yet to be kindled. Their personalities clashed during the long walk to school – and Abdullah would often run away before they even got there. How could Amal concentrate on her grades, when she always had to be checking up on Abdullah? She was beginning to feel thwarted in her aspirations.

In fact Amal's schooling was never really completed. When she was around fourteen, the opportunity arose for her to go to school in neighbouring Lebanon. But Hannah had other ideas – and hid her suitcase! When it was eventually found, halfway up the mountain and in a tree, it was too late. Amal had become increasingly valuable to her mother at home. In spite of her best intentions of seeking a structured education in the wider world, Amal was developing a gift for looking after her little brothers!

As if to strengthen her own argument for hanging on to her daughter, Hannah did manage to find some home tuition for Amal, and a high school graduate arrived from Tripoli. But for the majority of the time Amal helped her mother around the home. It became her job to fetch the water, wash the family clothes, and bathe her brothers. And as if that were not enough, two other little boys from a neighbouring family also needed looking after.

She helped her mother in the kitchen, learning how to turn the *burghal* or bulgar wheat into the breads and pancakes which were the staple of the area. The wheat arrived in sackloads, brought up from the farms on the plain on the backs of donkeys. Amal was developing the physical strength of the country-dweller, and would often help alongside the men in heaving the sacks off the donkeys and into the home.

Amal's capacity for ingenuity and hard work was already beginning to show itself. It was difficult for her to avoid the conclusion she was treated differently not only from her brothers, but from her three older sisters also. One possibility certainly did not occur to her, but might be queried by an onlooker: could it be she was already being groomed for the single daughter's life at home?

# Chapter Four

## *Al Kafroun*

Amal's range of talents was remarkable – not unlike her mother's, at a similar age. There were packs of grey wolves roaming the mountains, and the community's relationship with them was one of mutual stand-off; occasionally however the hungry pack leader would risk the farmer's gun, and slip through to the chickens, if not to something larger. The night-time wolf howls did not usually alert the family – but early one morning other animal noises certainly did. The family rushed out into the cold half-light of dawn, straining their eyes to try and make out what had happened: for one goat they only just got there in time. It appeared to be dead, but on closer examination there was still life there, the goat having suffered a massive tear to its abdomen. Aided by Hayat and Abdullah who held the goat down, it was Amal who managed to stitch the goat together again!

*I used ordinary needle and thread, sterilised with iodine – and it took just eight sutures!*

Another threat throughout the Middle East at that time was the ubiquitous malaria. For the most part immunity was maintained after the first flu-like attack, but occasionally the more deadly form struck.

Early on in Amal's school years, she suddenly became very ill.

*I was swelling up; none of my clothes fitted, so they put me in my sister's.*

Rapidly deteriorating into kidney failure, she was so ill that her parents decided they must get her to a hospital; her father propped her on one of the donkeys, then rode with her the several days' journey to the Presbyterian Hospital in Tripoli.

The family gathered, and everyone took turns by her bed. Gradually despair began to get a grip, as nothing seemed to be working; before their eyes she was slipping into a coma. Was there really no hope? But then Antonius' strong faith came to the fore. He turned to a friend of his, an Armenian Christian doctor at the hospital, and together they agreed to fast and pray. What followed could be explained no other way: a miraculous recovery had taken place.

*Somehow I managed to sit up, and call to the nurses that I was hungry. I pulled the needles and catheters out of my body, and demanded food.*

Amal never had kidney problems again.

It was becoming clear that, as much as her thoughts turned constantly to furthering her own education, Amal loved children.

When she was about ten, her oldest sister's first baby was born. The little girl became a special delight to Amal – a delicate treasure in the midst of a houseful of rumbustious young boys. If she wanted any reward after the prosaic nappy-washing, it was the privilege of wrapping the swaddling bands, rocking the cradle and getting her little charge back to sleep.

But then one day, when the baby was just four months old, she suddenly developed a severe fever. It quickly proved to be measles, which the family knew only too well was often fatal. They watched and waited, and did what they could: was she too hot? Too cold? Why was she shivering now? Somehow, in spite of some desperate efforts, her life seemed to slip through their fingers – and the blow, when it came, was massive. Amal was devastated; it seared through her hitherto childlike construct of life.

*We sang hymns as we walked through the olive groves to the church service – but I cried all the way.*

But it did start Amal thinking. Often she wandered alone back through the olive groves, picking wild flowers as she went, to put on the little grave. Where do people go when they die? Amal's thoughts strayed through new dimensions as she made the best of her flower arrangement. She had long talks with her father which turned her preoccupation increasingly to the after-life. She even found herself strangely looking forward to it. Antonius confidently told her that she would see her little niece again.

Amal's self-questioning grew deeper. Why did God seem far away? What was this personal relationship with the Almighty which others seemed to claim? Her sister Lydia had been talking about this for some months now; it had clearly made a difference to her life.

That Easter, Amal's existential questionings felt as if they were coming to a head. Lydia, still full of the joy of having become a 'believer' the previous year, was back from school in Tripoli for the holidays. On the Good Friday evening, the weather outside being unusually stormy, the family gathered together round an open fire. Amal, always scared of storms, clung extra tightly to another new little niece, Rajaa's first baby, cradled on her lap.

Before Antonius opened the family Bible, they joined together in singing a hymn. They sang about the cross, and the suffering of Christ – then Antonius read the account of the crucifixion from St Luke.

*Suddenly it struck me – how easily Christ gave in to be
killed. He could have done something – but he didn't.
Why? I started to cry, as silently as I could, hiding behind
my sister's baby.*

Antonius closed the gathering with a prayer, and everyone disappeared off to bed. But Amal couldn't sleep.

Morning eventually came, relieving Amal of one of the most restless nights she had ever spent. Her mind had been in turmoil throughout the darkest hours. What was the purpose of her life? What was it really all about? In the morning she took a Bible with her on a walk down to the bottom of the garden, sat herself down under one of the pomegranate trees, and began to read. She started from the beginning of the Gospel of Luke. Knowing the stories so well, she forced herself to read slowly and carefully. She came to the story of the two thieves.

Suddenly – her moment of truth flooded in. She found herself kneeling on the prickly grass, tears flowing.

*God opened my mind and heart, and I understood why he died. I asked him to save me, just as he had saved the dying thief.*

As if in one movement Amal shot to her feet and ran back to the house; she called out to anyone who was listening, announcing what had happened. She was deliriously happy – and what's more, she knew she would never be afraid of storms again.

Very soon her friends began to notice the difference in her; the smile seemed to remain on her face all day – even when she was bringing back the heavy water-pot from the spring. Straight away Amal began the habit which would characterise the rest of her life – she felt compelled to tell people why she was so happy.

But she longed to prove, to herself if to no-one else, that a change really had taken place within her.

Amal had been brought up to handle animals very confidently – sometimes a bit too confidently, she thought. She felt she could be rough, and decided this was an area in which she could show everyone she was a changed person. One day her opportunity came.

Everyone seemed busy outside; a spare pair of hands was needed to manage the new calf, which had to be kept away from its mother, so the cow could be milked. The job was given to Amal – but she was preoccupied; her mind only half on the task in hand, she wandered off absent-mindedly to pick figs. Suddenly she was brought back to reality – where was the calf? She realised that in her brief lapse, the calf had made its way back to its mother; she grabbed a stone, intending to scare the calf off in the opposite direction. But to her horror she hit the calf on the head. Immediately it fell down – and lay awfully still; in fact it was bleeding from its ear. The implication flooded in to Amal's horror-struck mind. In that split second she feared more for the fact they would not believe she had changed, than for the fate of the calf. Nevertheless, even as she cried out to God to heal, and if necessary resurrect, the calf... the calf got up.

As Amal settled to her new relationship with God, and consequent new sense of purpose in life, she spent long periods alone with her Bible. She particularly studied the letters of St Paul, and began consciously to model herself on the great Apostle. At the same time she found herself drawn to the idea of a medical career – but she also began to realise people needed healing on the inside.

# Chapter Five

## *Beirut & Gaza*

In 1946, when Amal was sixteen, the opportunity again arose for her to go to Lebanon. The circumstances were different this time however; this was not for her own education, but for that of her two youngest brothers, the *Kafroun* school having closed down. Suppressing the notion that her own education was once again being marginalised for the sake of that of her male siblings, she began to look forward to this shift in her horizons. She was older also of course, so now there was no question, Hannah must let her daughter go.

Amal, Raja and Robert stayed in the home of Amal's sister Hayat and her English husband, in Beirut. In fact Robert was still only four years old, so for much of the time Amal was at home with him, while seven-year-old Raja went to school. They were there for the whole of the school year.

Fashionable Beirut took Amal's breath away. Sleek modern vehicles blew their horns as they raced along the Corniche; French boutiques, mouth-watering patisseries and upmarket bars lined the water-front: here men and women mixed together, sitting and sipping wine among the pungent hookahs – this stylish resort on the Syria/Lebanon coast was the pearl of the eastern Mediterranean, and now the War was over, wealthy tourists were flocking in.

It was all far more sophisticated than anything Amal had ever seen.

There was beauty too in the hills surrounding the city, green until the parched summer months arrived. Looking impossibly steep, they were nevertheless terraced with palatial Ottoman architecture, and with just a hint of fragrant cedar forests beyond.

Predictably however for a sensitive teenager it was the experience of flush toilets which made the strongest impression!

And there were challenges also: she soon discovered you certainly do not pass the time of day with everyone in a city, as you did at home. This could definitely lead to trouble. And sophistication, she soon realised, brought other hazards.

*It was seeing naked people that put me off Beirut.*

Long associated in Arab eyes with Western decadence, this strange idea made her feel particularly uncomfortable. Swimming in the sea was something Amal loved however, so running the gauntlet of bodies flaunting barely adequate swimwear, she spent any available free time on the beach.

It was the ubiquitous tea vendors and shoe-shine boys that gave her a more familiar feel. And the beggars too caught her compassionate eye. She noticed that whereas the majority Muslim and Christian communities were influential in business and government, it was the minority Druze community which usually constituted the poor and marginalised of the city.

And as she walked the bustling cosmopolitan streets she gradually became aware of another influence – that of the foreign Christian missions. As with the American Presbyterians in Tripoli, they were responsible for much of the education and healthcare in the area. Amal made a point of linking up with one particular group, the British Syrian Mission. Responsible for schools popular with both Muslims and Christians, as well as a teacher training college and a school for the blind, they also seemed to be the ones who were doing the most for the Druze.

It was through her association with this mission that she also became acquainted with the presence of a new phenomenon, that of the Palestinian refugees.

Amal returned home after twelve months with her head reeling. She had seen firsthand the fruits of successful commerce and fashionable enterprise; she knew she had enjoyed herself – but at the same time the backstreet poverty had left its mark on her impressionable conscience.

Meanwhile her sister Lydia had been having life-changing experiences also. She had embarked on a course at the Bible School in Tripoli, and that summer of 1947, as she and others graduated, some adventurous plans for the future were formulated. As she set off home, Lydia mulled over what she was beginning to feel God wanted her to do. She decided she would share her plans with Amal. There was a certain hospital in Gaza which desperately needed help apparently – could the two of them think of going there together?

But what on earth were their parents going to say?

So now for the second time Amal was confronted with the plight of the Palestinian refugees. In the late-night conversations with Lydia, Amal's vivid imagination kicked in; she recalled the desperate state of the newly arrived Palestinians, dazed and rootless on the streets of Beirut. For decades now Jews had been 'returning' to Palestine from around the world, for the most part successfully integrating alongside the Palestinian inhabitants. But now Zionists were encouraging an increase in these moves, with plans to provide the Jews with a specific homeland – one that would be called Israel.

Palestinians were allocated a greatly diminished area to call their own, and many living in the newly-designated Israeli areas fled as refugees, some to other countries, some to their allocated areas, one of which was the Gaza Strip.

Amal's spirit soared at the thought of the challenge. One thing was sure – she wanted to go.

Amal's mother Hannah had not wanted Amal to go to school; she had not really wanted her to go anywhere; and she certainly wasn't going to support this latest hair-brained do-gooding idea. She decided to hide their passports. As the critical time of departure drew near, Hannah was nowhere to be found: she had disappeared off to stay with some friends in a nearby village, taking the passports with her. She returned after what looked rather like a three-day sulk – having fasted and cut her hair. But her stricken appearance, if it was meant to work on her girls, had no effect. There were massive arguments, even fighting, both girls losing clumps of hair in the process. But they gained their precious passports, took their opportunity and slipped away – while Hannah again disappeared off to the home of her friends. In spite of everything Lydia and Amal were deeply saddened at the thought they had not been able to say goodbye to their mother – but the anticipation of their first aeroplane journey bucked their spirits, and deepest joy of all for Amal, she was beginning to follow her dream.

Medical volunteers were pouring into Gaza – but so were Palestinian refugees, and in far greater numbers. At her first sight of a UN refugee camp, Amal had to strain her eyes into the distance: the camp-sites consisted of row upon orderly row of tents, reaching out across the flat parched coastal plain as far as the eye could see.

But Amal was in a group of twenty destined for the English Hospital (later to become *Al Ahli* Arab Hospital) in over-stretched Gaza City. Some of the group were doctors and nurses; Lydia's official role, in this Christian hospital, was that of missionary Bible teacher; Amal, the youngest in the group, was 'just' a volunteer.

*We had so much work to do. I worked like a horse.*

She threw herself into the work of the following months. While Lydia led Bible studies, and talked to the patients in the waiting areas, Amal was helping to wash and care for those who were bed-bound. Many of the refugees had horrific injuries from landmines, and Amal became acquainted with unpleasant sights and smells, and desperately sad stories.

*I learnt to talk to the dying; and I began to see God answer prayer quickly.*

The patients grew very fond of her, some calling her the Arab Nightingale.

Each day finished with weariness – but there was something else. She was too tired to think about it at first, but every now and again it would catch her: a sudden flush of sheer delight when she was least expecting it. It left a deep contentment which Amal put down to a sense of fulfilment; this was her understanding of God's will for her at this stage of her life. She was so happy she even caught herself singing a hymn sometimes, on her way to fetch the water from the hospital well. This was her calling, and as far as she was concerned she would be doing this, or something very like it, for the rest of her life.

And when it came to time off, once again it was the sparkle of the Mediterranean which beckoned. Sometimes as a team, sometimes in ones and twos, they took the bus to the sea-front, and unwound from their varying responsibilities with swimming, and picnics on the vast near-deserted sandy beach.

As time went on, Amal was given the opportunity to learn new skills: she received training in how to give vaccinations. She saw this as another step forward into her medical destiny; as it turned out it was going to be of enormous help also in her next experience.

So after about a year, other horizons began to beckon. Lydia and Amal went their separate ways, Lydia to join Middle East Christian Outreach, working throughout the region, and for a while Amal returned home.

...back home in Al Kafroun

# Chapter Six

## *Damascus*

After a few months at home, and now approaching eighteen, Amal was restless again.

Her sister Hayat and family had relocated to Damascus, where Hayat was working as a translator for the Ministry of Health. Rajaa the middle sister was working there also, employed by the United Nations; both sisters suggested Amal might like to come and stay, and possibly find work among the growing Palestinian refugee population. When Amal found out that Rajaa was actually engaged in feeding and vaccination programmes, her heart leapt. After all, she had been trained to give vaccinations!

As she set off for Damascus, Amal found herself wondering if she might just end up looking after her sisters' children. Much as they loved her, and she knew she was well suited, she also felt something much more significant was beckoning.

Damascus itself was the capital of her home country; it was near to home, and did not present either the extreme challenge of Gaza, or the cultural shocks of Beirut.

*There were no naked people in Damascus.*

It was not nearly so difficult for her mother to accept either – and of course there had been no need for passport tussles.

Nevertheless, much as her father had been in Tripoli, so many years before, Amal was at first mesmerised by her new surroundings. Here were no seascapes or broad horizons. Within the city walls of Damascus lay a labyrinth of narrow streets; in places almost like tunnels, their cantilevered upper storeys were so close as to be nearly touching: inhabitants could talk to one another from house to house.

Amal wandered through the ancient *Al Hamidiyah* souk, watching silks and sumptuous carpets being haggled over, and old items of silver and brassware changing hands. There were the shop fronts with gleaming glass cabinets displaying beguiling gold jewellery – beguiling that is except for someone of a no-nonsense and unadorned disposition such as Amal; she was more drawn to the sweetmeats and crystallised fruits. And everywhere, and strangely penetrating even the din of bartering and trade, the constant tap-tap-tapping of the coppersmiths could be heard.

The magnificence of the *Umayyad* Mosque, with its intricate minarets and arches, held limited fascination; Amal was more interested in the fact there had been a church on the same site for centuries before the mosque; many of the original pillars and features of the church were incorporated in the 'new' building. The head of John the Baptist was also supposed to be buried there – but relics didn't interest Amal.

The smell of jasmine was everywhere: the gardens couldn't be seen, tucked away within the hidden courtyards of the houses, but the fountains could be heard – and they wafted the scent of the jasmine over the walls, refreshing the hot air which blew in through the gates of the city on the sand-laden desert winds.

Amal found work with the UN Relief and Works Agency alongside Rajaa. Most of the health workers were from Scandinavia, and Amal was shadowing a group of Danish nurses.

The cramped conditions in which most refugees lived gave a head start to diseases such as tuberculosis, and a massive vaccination programme was underway. Before the vaccination comes the test, however, and Amal was delighted to add a new skill to her repertoire: before long she was adept with the comparatively painless but horrific sounding Heaf-gun, used to administer the Mantoux test via a circle of six tiny needles applied to the skin of the patient's lower arm. The result is 'read' after three days, and if negative, the BCG vaccination has to be given.

With no beautiful beach to summon her, time off in Damascus was obviously going to take a different turn. For companionship Amal once again sought out the British Syrian Mission, as she had done when at a loose end on the streets of Beirut. Here too the Mission was hard at work in the sphere of education: they ran a girls' school, and it happened to be situated on Straight Street, of New Testament fame. This held special significance for Amal, with its association with St Paul, one of her biblical heroes. Straight Street was so-called as it ran straight as an arrow from one side of the old city to the other; it is an unusually wide street also, wide enough for the Roman chariots of old – or now the French tramcars which were such a novelty to Amal.

One of the teachers at the girls' school was a Miss Stammers, an English missionary; although fifteen years older than Amal, Pauline Stammers nevertheless became a close and long-term friend. A group from the Mission made occasional evangelistic excursions into the surrounding villages; not surprisingly, when Pauline suggested she might like to join them, Amal jumped at the idea.

*We travelled out to the villages by bus. The men preached in the market-places, and I went with Pauline to visit the women in their homes.*

Amal got to know her new Christian friends during relaxed evening conversations; they sat together in the dark of the school courtyard, looking up at the inky black desert sky; or, more desperate to catch the evening breeze, a group of them would climb *Jebel Qasioun* to the north of the city; there, to the music of the cicadas, they would sit and watch the city lights come on.

Among other things she learnt they had all been baptised as adult believers; from her own Orthodox upbringing this seemed strange to Amal, who had been baptised as a baby. She had lots of questions to ask on the subject. And before going ahead she also had to assure herself she was not just trying to follow in St Paul's footsteps, he also having been baptised in this city. She became convinced, however, and early one morning, before it got too hot, a group of friends from the Mission gathered on the banks of the *Al Awaj* river. This just happens to be one of the rivers favoured by Naaman the Syrian in the Old Testament; he referred to it by its ancient name of Pharpar. Thousands of years on, and the rivers of Damascus are still delivering sparkling clean water from the Lebanese highlands, just as Naaman had remembered they did, when he was away in Israel. So this was where Amal was baptised, by the Egyptian pastor who worked with the Mission.

There was something else to which she found her mind returned with increasing frequency, something about Pauline which really made her think. Pauline was single, resolutely so it seemed to Amal; as much as she was known at times to delight in a spot of matchmaking on behalf of others, she actually seemed to enjoy her own single status. It was far too early for Amal to know yet of course, but might this be the way things would work out, a calling perhaps, for her also?

Such thoughts were quickly pushed to the back of her mind in the busyness of each day. The successful anti-TB campaign was continuing outside the refugee camps of Damascus, and on into the school population –

*We did nearly every school in Damascus.*

– and thence south to *Jebel al Arab*, the mountainous southern region towards the Jordanian border where at one time the Druze had their own autonomous state.

Here Amal was back within a remote village setting reminiscent of her childhood – back with narrow mountain paths (maintained as such by the Druze, for reasons of defence), and back with water only from springs, unlike Damascus which had enjoyed abundant piped water for twenty or thirty years. She felt at home here, and found she was cultivating the sensitivities needed to develop close and trusting relationships with the village women. She related well to each one, sometimes with deep compassion.

In these more remote villages of the southern desert regions the women were even more modest than their city counterparts. Amal, whose own modesty was beyond reproach, was able to identify with this. She appreciated that, as well as being understandably resistant to the anticipated shock of the vaccination, the women's ingrained modesty made it difficult for them to expose even their upper arm. Amal worked out a way of maintaining that modesty; she designed a kind of screen behind which only she could view the potential vaccination site of the upper arm.

This seemingly small move assisted in the uptake of vaccinations and had immediate popular acclaim; it was even reported in the local newspapers, and Amal was awarded a prize for her excellent work at a special meal with local dignitaries.

'It's a pity you don't do nursing' was the oft-repeated comment now, from her Danish colleagues. So she and her sister Lydia, with whom she had travelled to Gaza, both applied for training in the Danish Mission Hospital in *Nabk*, halfway between Homs and Damascus.

But the early weeks were very practical, exploitative even, with lots of cleaning more than hands-on patient care. This upset Lydia, more than the resilient Amal, who was always ready to roll up her sleeves – so after just six months they returned home.

But her enduring and treasured memory of *Nabk* was not so much the gleaming white hospital itself, the airy corridors or the sun-baked walled garden; it was that she had had to read from the Bible every morning in the wards. Years later at a conference she heard someone sharing publicly their experience of having been a patient in that hospital. As a result of Amal's words, she said, she had become a Christian there.

*– She remembered me. I was so encouraged – just one in the six months!*

Amal began her training in the 1950s

# Chapter Seven

## *Aleppo & the Golan Heights*

But Amal of course was never going to give up that easily on what she was increasingly coming to believe was her life's vocation. And very soon, and again within the borders of Syria, she found the place which did suit her, for the next stage in her life.

It was now 1951, and Amal was twenty-one years old. She had arrived in Aleppo, Syria's northern metropolis.

Just fifty kilometres from the Turkish border, Aleppo lies at the heart of the Middle East, and was at one time the foremost city in the region. For hundreds of years it built up a sumptuous range of Roman, Christian and Ottoman architecture. With the largest Christian population of any Middle Eastern city up until the Second World War it was known among other things as the City of Cathedrals. Decades before, with the opening of the Suez Canal it lost its superior trading position at the end of the Silk Road: exotic silks and spices had to give way to the more local olives and pistachios.

By Aleppo standards the Altounian Hospital was a modern building. It was founded in 1912 by Dr Aram Altounian, who was himself trained at the American Hospital in Gaziantep across the modern-day border in Turkey; from here he and his family had fled south to Aleppo to escape the Armenian massacre and forced marches, leading up to the First World War.

When Amal began her training there in the 1950s the hospital was still a rising star as far as medical facilities in the Middle East were concerned. She particularly enjoyed surgical nursing, and one of the surgeons she knew well was Ernest Altounian, Cambridge-trained and now back as a consultant in his family's hospital. This meant the hospital, as well as Christian in its foundation, was strongly linked with the UK. Medical students came and went from Britain on their 'electives', and new equipment and medicine from the West was in evidence. The Altounian family was also well-connected socially, and the hospital had gained a reputation among foreign dignitaries as somewhere to visit when 'passing through'; during Amal's time there was always the expectation that Agatha Christie and her archaeologist husband might just call in, fresh from a Mesopotamian dig, before spending the night nearby in the faded opulence of Aleppo's Baron Hotel.

It was also a good place to be treated. The hospital's standards were high – but it had gained something of a 'Robin Hood' reputation. Wealthy sheikhs and demanding Westerners alike were happy to pay for the privilege of being patients there; this in turn enabled the hospital to maintain its well-established philanthropic ethos: the Armenian collective memory of their own sufferings was such that they could never ignore the plight of the poor and marginalised in the backstreets of wherever they happened to be in the world. This all sat very comfortably with Amal; her own sense of compassion – responsibility almost – for those less privileged, was developing into a motivating force.

The hospital complex, which survived until the early years of the twenty-first century, was situated in the newly-developing Azizieh district of Aleppo. The geometric layout of the immediate area, with its wide boulevards and well-made roads, was perfect for increasingly speedy forms of transport. Many of the more established members of the hospital staff had cars, so escape out of Aleppo, out into the shady walnut groves for group picnics, or into the surrounding desert in all but the hottest months, was a popular way of spending time off. A longer but favoured drive took them as far as the Euphrates. The river snaked its way down from the Turkish border through miles of barren landscape, glistening like mercury in the shimmering heat; in dramatic contrast there were places where the river banks were lush and green; this gave welcome shade, and made the long, hot car journey worthwhile.

And it was here, at some point during her training, when Amal came close to death for the second time in her life. It was before the lunchtime picnic, and some of the group had decided to go for a swim.

*Everyone knew I could never resist water.*

Amal, the soul of discretion, had taken the precaution of putting her costume on under her clothes. But when it came to it even this was not enough – she was not going to remove so much as a stitch of clothing in front of any audience, and today particularly as she was in a mixed party; so to get away from everyone she went along the river, further upstream, to a place where no-one could see. Here the bushes along the river bank satisfied her modesty. The trouble was, when it came to diving in she was still comparatively hidden – and very much alone. Nevertheless, unhesitating, she plunged into the irresistibly cool water. Almost immediately she realised she was not in control; her well-honed swimming skills were just not having any effect; the current was taking over, so she started shouting, at the same time desperately trying to grab the overhanging branches – which seemed to be passing her by at alarming speed. In the end two people managed to drag her out – one of whom was the hospital director!

The majority of her time at the Altounian passed with far less drama. Her four years there was the longest period of time she had spent in any one place since she first left home. The first year was a full-time English and foundation studies course. English, essential for medical study, was already a preferred second language as far as many younger Syrians were concerned.

Then came the three-year nursing course; Amal did well in her studies, gaining a prize at the end of the course.

But the sophisticated life of this modern and prestigious hospital was beginning to pall. The link with the UK had fascinated her, and had dovetailed in with her increasing proficiency in English; it also left her wondering for the first time what life outside the Middle East was really like. But as graduation approached, Amal felt the call of more challenging horizons once again. She had been reminded of the ongoing plight of the Palestinian refugees, this time on the Golan Heights.

As soon as she had completed her studies therefore, she took her leave of Aleppo – and headed to *Qunaitra*, at the foot of the Golan Heights. *Qunaitra* itself, like so many of Syria's cities, currently retained much of its Ottoman elegance, having prospered for so long as part of the caravan route from Palestine north to Turkey and thence to the Silk Road; it had yet to suffer its destruction at the hands of Israel in the Six-Day War of 1967.

Here Amal linked up with the UN Relief and Works Agency once again, the organisation formed in response to the Palestinian refugee crisis which she had worked with in Damascus. Now qualified, she was working at a higher level of responsibility, and she loved this. As well as clinical work she was now responsible for dispensing advice, teaching the refugees on a variety of health-related subjects. Dietary advice, along with food hygiene and preparation, were important areas; with her Arabic roots she was better-placed than some of the Western medics when it came to knowing what would or would not be acceptable to Palestinian palates. She was based at a clinic, but preferred travelling round – together with a pharmacist she was regularly driven out to the refugee camps. Here among the tents, converted container-dwellings and fly-blown latrines she felt most at home. She treated minor injuries and ailments, as well as managing the vaccination programmes – and she loved being surrounded by the ubiquitous crowds of children.

*Here I was very, very happy; I didn't want to leave.*

The days flew by, and once again Amal, if she had time to think about it at all, felt that deep sense of purpose, and 'rightness' about what she was doing. She remembered how fulfilled she had felt at times back in Gaza as a teenager. She rarely thought of the future – but if she did, she was sure it would be spent here.

But much to her disappointment this was not going to be. After Amal had been there for only a year, it was suddenly announced that the camp was going to be closed down. Palestinians would have to re-distribute themselves to any one of the increasing number of camps that were becoming a permanent feature throughout the Middle East. The UN also would have to move on; they were responsible only for relief work, not in any way for the political status of the camps. And it was back to the drawing board for Amal.

Meanwhile her sister Rajaa had qualified as a nurse in the British hospital in Beirut, and had found work in Saudi Arabia. Would Amal like to join her? This would be a strange next move for Amal. Christians were not welcome in Saudi Arabia – the expatriate community had to keep their faith very much to themselves, and this was not Amal's way – neither was she particularly attracted to the idea of moving back into the more high-powered echelons of medicine. Yet she needed to find work. The decision she made to resign from the UN and join her sister proved to be pivotal: it would enable her to meet the person who would point her in the direction she was destined to take for the rest of her life.

...could never resist water

# Chapter Eight

## *Saudi Arabia*

So in 1956, and after a disappointingly short time in *Qunaitra*, Amal went to join her sister Rajaa in Saudi Arabia.

Impossibly vast, and veiled in mystery as far as most of the outside world was concerned, the Kingdom of Saudi Arabia had recently discovered oil; very soon it would be beginning its transformation from primitive Bedouin backwater to a place of gleaming skyscrapers, hospitals, universities – even proper pavements.

Riyadh, the capital city, had none of the old world familiarity Amal had so far encountered throughout the Middle East. Immediately she missed the historic Christian foundations, both architectural and political, which so pervaded Syria, Lebanon, even Palestine. The heat was different here too – and the dress code, even the accent...but above all the spiritual atmosphere.

*The prayer call closed the shops – and there was no*
*walking around the streets during prayers.*
*Saudi was dark! It felt like Islam in its worst form.*

Nevertheless Amal buckled down to all the challenges; her skirts became floor-length, and she draped a scarf over her head. She was relieved she did not have to wear stockings!

With her usual mixture of stoic commitment and an almost childlike sense of enjoyment Amal stayed in her first post, in Defence Hospital, Riyadh, for a two-year contract, working in what was known as the operating room. This was not so much operating theatre as emergency room – where minor surgical procedures and emergency treatments were carried out. After the first year Rajaa returned home to Syria.

Amal, content in her chosen area of nursing, continued for the second year.

When this came to an end, almost immediately Amal was offered a further two-year contract, in another military hospital but this time across on the other side of the country.

The so-called summer capital of Saudi Arabia, *Ta'if* is situated in the cooler mountainous region along the Red Sea coast. This was an obvious incentive to Amal, who was only too pleased to take her leave of the city of Riyadh, trapped in the burning white heat of Saudi's central plain. Additionally she was offered an enhanced role – that of interpreter. English was the medium in which medicine was practised – indeed many of the staff were themselves from the West; but many of the patients were Arabic-only speakers, and so the role of interpreter between the two was at times critical.

Eventually her time in *Ta'if* came to an end. Amal applied for one more posting; in terms of her future life path, this would be by far the most significant of the three.

The Arabian American Oil Company (ARAMCO), founded in New York in 1933, soon afterwards established its headquarters at Dhahran on the east coast of Saudi Arabia, where the US were successful in finding oil. In 1951 that success was increased, as yet more oil was found offshore: the Americans would definitely be around for a while! They settled in to build a small city for themselves, and soon they had houses and schools, their own TV station, even an English language newspaper aptly named *Sun and Flare*. And of course there was a hospital, the Dhahran Health Center. By the time Amal had arrived in 1960, it could already lay claim to some scientific successes. Malaria, endemic there for as long as anyone could remember, had been a particular problem for expatriate workers with their absence of acquired immunity. In collaboration with the Saudi government, ARAMCO was responsible for launching a massive anti-malarial campaign in 1956. Malaria was successfully eradicated in Saudi Arabia largely by intensive house-spraying in the region.

Then there was the desperate search for a cure for trachoma, a disease causing blindness, which was particularly prevalent throughout the Middle East and the Gulf. Just before Amal arrived, the Aramco Trachoma Research Program was set up, and it was progressing both in terms of isolating the virus for a possible vaccine, and in determining a cure.

These two major achievements had enhanced the reputation of Dhahran Health Center throughout the Gulf region.

As time went on the enormous gated community developed by the Americans became less exclusive, with increasing facilities for the Saudi and other workers. When Amal arrived, however, it was still perceived as something of a refuge, with a sense of isolation from the effects of strict Islamic law, and with, on the positive side, a fair degree of Western comfort thrown in. The overall atmosphere was very American. If she were so disposed, Amal could follow the excitement of the basket-ball league, watch the latest 'movies', or join a drama group; she could attend beach parties and dinner dances, or try her hand at anything from water-colouring to shark-fishing. Strangely none of these things was to Amal's taste. She had other things on her mind.

The base at 'Aramco', being American, was therefore 'Christian'. Here there was complete freedom to worship, with plenty of activity going on in the various churches. Amal's first Christmas there was dominated by an epic nativity play: with a cast of forty-six, plus almost impossible numbers of real live camels, donkeys, sheep and goats, and an audience of over a thousand, its authenticity was rescued by the fact it was staged under a starry Middle Eastern sky.

But even this, both moving and entertaining as it was, did not attract Amal's attention as much as the Christian conferences which occasionally took place. Well-known speakers from other parts of the world were often flown in, and Amal found a spiritual thirst within her was beginning to be quenched. She had always loved studying the Bible, and was eager to hear those who were able to expound its depths and clarify her queries.

In those days a female speaker still raised a few eyebrows; when the famous Dr Sarah Hosman, veteran American missionary working in the Trucial States (as the UAE was then known), strode onto the platform, there was hushed silence. This was not just a woman, but a woman who had had a hospital named after her.

The appearance of this nearly eighty-year-old speaker, bespectacled, earnest-looking, and with severely outmoded dress-sense, was incredibly imposing. She had a distinctive limp – yet this did not detract from her bearing. She spoke with grave authority – but Amal was not intimidated: as far as she was concerned this woman had something important to say.

*I liked her. I was also invited to assist her, as she was so old.*

This was it. This was Amal's opportunity. As she accompanied the revered Doctor to the dining area, then the 'rest-room', then back to the conference room again, she made the most of her undivided time with someone who she felt held the key to the direction of her life from now on. Amal summoned up her courage.

*I asked her if she had any freedom to witness in the Gulf. Yes, she replied: in midwifery you become much closer to the woman.*

Her affirmative answer was due to very specific circumstances.

Dr Hosman, a qualified obstetrician, had been working in the Gulf since 1914. She started her work in Oman, and then from 1939 for some years she itinerated on the back of a mule throughout the Trucial States. She later set up a mobile clinic – but most of her deliveries took place either in stone-built desert huts, in homes constructed with lumps of coral in the coastal communities, or very often in tents.

In 1951 however the Sheikh of Ajman's wife was ill. It appeared Dr Hosman saved her life, whereupon in gratitude, and in awareness of the poor state of maternity care in his country, the Sheikh invited her to stay and open a hospital in one of his spare palaces. Dr Hosman could drive a hard bargain: she insisted on having written permission to share the Gospel within its walls. Thus the Sarah Hosman Hospital of Sharjah came into being.

Amal was drawn into this remarkable lady's story. Arab desert hospitality, she knew, involved floor cushions, not tables and chairs. The beds would all be low also. How on earth did she manage? Amal had discovered during the course of the conference that Dr Hosman's limp was due to the fact she had an artificial (wooden in those days) leg. She had had this major handicap since a childhood accident. How did she cope in those basic huts and tented dwellings, let alone on the back of a mule?!

Amal felt she had just stumbled on both a fascinating story, and her own destiny.

In fact she had first encountered midwifery when she was in Riyadh. Not qualified herself as such, she had nevertheless assisted the midwives and obstetricians when they had been delivering the babies of the many members of the Saudi royal family. She remembered helping with the wives of Crown Prince Fahad while they were in the hospital. (The Crown Prince had become known to the British public when he represented his country at the Queen's coronation in 1953. When Amal met him he was still Crown Prince, and Minister of the Interior – he became King in 1982.)

So her time in Aramco, Dhahran, was coming to an end. She knew midwifery training, possibly in the West, was the next step. And she knew she would then return to the poor people, amongst whom she loved to be, somewhere within the Middle East.

Apart from anything else she would never earn anywhere near so much money again. She had faithfully sent money home to her parents in Syria – but her non-frivolous lifestyle had enabled her to save also. She had been told London would be the best place for her training: it would be expensive, she surmised – but she was prepared.

So she wrote to various London hospitals; she also wrote to her English friend from Damascus days, Pauline Stammers. Pauline's own roots were in southern England; because this was where she returned when on 'furlough', Amal wanted her to know she herself was planning on coming to London. Pauline suggested the Mothers' Hospital in East London as being right for Amal.

She was at a turning point in other ways. She would for the first time be leaving behind the Arab world, and the culture and people with which she was most familiar. Now well past thirty, she was also taking a step back from the inevitability of marriage; she had even had a proposal from a Saudi man – which she turned down. Her little brothers were now marrying – soon she would be the only one among her siblings still single – still without that assumed passport to respectability and status which marriage almost by default, and certainly within Arab culture, seems to provide. Would she feel marginalised, socially irrelevant, in comparison? Amal refused to let any such thoughts intrude on the excitement of this next stage.

...deliveries took place in stone-built desert huts

# Chapter Nine

## *London*

Amal was offered a place for midwifery training at the Mothers' Hospital in East London, starting September 1963. Having acted on Pauline's suggestion, and been successful, she never furthered her enquiries anywhere else. She flew straight from Dhahran in the August, touching down in the newly Beatle-crazed UK, at Heathrow Airport.

*I was collected from the airport in a car and taken straight to the hospital. I liked it straight away.*

It must have been the garden, with flowers and trees and even a pond, which first captivated Amal's eye, as the hospital, situated on Lower Clapton Road, was set back behind some rather forbidding railings, with two enormous brick pillars either side of the gate through which she was driven. The tall imposing Georgian buildings had once been homes for the wealthy of fashionable Hackney. Having gathered more than a hundred years-worth of soot and grime, however, they now presented a dark and somewhat depressing façade; Amal just speculated that perhaps the whole of London were like this. But the place was transformed in her eyes as she walked through the archway between these buildings. Here were the wards, newer, purpose-built and set out bungalow style, the traditional 'cottage hospital' effect. They were connected by open verandahs, and between the wards and verandahs were the well-kept gardens – an oasis in the midst of London's bustling and raucous East End. And between the flower-beds was an abundance of cherry trees; they were just beginning to glow with the colours of autumn, with the promise of a riot of blossom for the following spring.

The Mothers' Hospital was founded and run by the Salvation Army as part of their social provision, initially for unmarried mothers. It had become part of the NHS in 1948, but retained its distinctive Christian ethos. In the 1960s many on the staff were still either Salvation Army officers, or active within the Army; they still saw the hospital as 'God's work' (although increasingly this had to be balanced, in some eyes at least, with the fact it was 'government work').

But the women of the East End, in spite of being from an incredible variety of cultural and religious backgrounds, rarely complained, or asked to be excluded, when morning prayers and a Bible reading took place on the wards. On Sundays the service was slightly longer – with a 'talk'. Also after every delivery a prayer of thanksgiving was said by the midwife – this also was rarely refused.

Amal settled quickly in her plain little room within the lofty buildings at the front of the hospital.

The full course to become a qualified midwife was usually just one year, the latter half of which was mainly work 'on the district'. It was assumed that those who had gained their general nursing qualification within the UK had some obstetric experience. This included Amal: she had a certificate proving three months' basic training in the maternity unit in Riyadh. Nevertheless her qualifications and experience gained in Syria and Saudi somehow were not quite enough: her training was extended to almost two years. Amal found this extremely frustrating. Much as she came to love midwifery, with its close involvement with the mothers at a vulnerable time in their lives, she did not want to delay unnecessarily her progress, and eventual return to the Middle East.

There were other frustrations. Amal had come from positions carrying responsibility and respect; now her tendency towards being outspoken suddenly had a different backdrop, in the starched atmosphere of ward hierarchy, or the classroom deference given to some consultant egos. She once interrupted a lecturer who happened to refer to the evolutionary process. Amal was resistant to any reference to evolution – word got back to the sister tutor, and Amal was in trouble – but it was far from the last time she would be outspoken.

With her international experience, Amal was usually at ease with cross-cultural relationships, even if not with hierarchical ones. She soon discovered, however, that she had not factored in the strict attitudes to alcohol within both the Salvation Army, and some other Protestant church groupings. A German colleague spotted the fact Amal sometimes had a bottle of wine in her room. She was quite clear on her stance on this, however, ably pointing out that, according to the Bible, Christians are allowed to drink wine: it is getting drunk which is forbidden.

But the patients, both the mothers and the newborn babies, were her delight.

The majority of patients seemed to be from the Irish and Jamaican communities. There were also many from the large East End Jewish population. A rabbi used to come to the hospital, to circumcise the little boys on the eighth day.

Amal had a particular heart for the unmarried mothers, many of them pitiably young. They were segregated from the 'ordinary' mothers – although if there were any possibility they might marry, they were encouraged to do so before registering the birth. Many of their babies were for adoption.

*I had mixed feelings as I watched these teenage girls bond with their babies during the ten days they were with us.*

The Salvation Army had done sterling work among unmarried mothers, with many Homes dedicated to their care. The nearest to the Mothers' Hospital was *Crossways*, in Stoke Newington. This is where the girls came from when they were in labour, and returned to afterwards, with or without their baby.

Amongst the verandahs and bungalows which made up the hospital there was a state-of-the-art premature baby unit. Known somewhat forbiddingly as Block Six, inside it was nevertheless warm and cheery, with the very latest style of incubator. In those days it was still considered best with the 'prems' to keep cuddling and human contact to a minimum – another precept with which Amal struggled! It also meant these babies were often fed in their incubator.

The fathers, if there were any, were discouraged from hanging around or handling their babies, for fear of infection – they were certainly not present at the birth – a new-fangled idea not due to take hold until the end of the sixties.

Not of a shy disposition, Amal enjoyed the mix of nationalities who were training alongside her – a mix as varied as that amongst the patients.

*I made friends quickly, particularly with the Canadians and Jamaicans.*

They for their part quickly warmed to this slightly older colleague with attractive dark curly hair and ready sense of fun, and a fund of stories from a little-known part of the world. They were bemused that someone whose approach to clinical standards was perfectly scientific, could sit of an evening and get into an argument about one of her many conspiracy theories: there surely had to be, for example, a more plausible explanation for the tides than just the phases of the moon!

With her new friends, or sometimes alone, she explored the local area, gradually widening her reach, either on the top of the red London buses, where she gazed down in fascination into people's back gardens, bracing herself for the slap on the windows from the passing tree branches; or else she rode what she considered to be the incredibly straightforward Underground system. London held no fears for Amal, and she wanted to experience everything it had to offer ('everything' of course being whatever lay within Amal's strict code of propriety).

The very local Chatsworth Road street market Amal discovered within the first week. She soon decided the cheap and brightly coloured plastic storage containers were every bit as useful and attractive as the more exotic wares found in Middle Eastern souks. She also enjoyed sophisticated Oxford Street, which had a very different pull.

Then there was swimming. Hackney Baths were just at the end of the road. As well as a bathhouse for those whose home plumbing had yet to be modernised, there were two indoor heated swimming pools, still resplendent with Victorian ironwork balconies and decorated tiles. But in summer the lido in nearby Victoria Park beckoned; like all London public open-air baths, it was free before nine o'clock every morning.

Whatever the weather, Amal got out and about, whenever her duties or studies allowed. Her new friends were amazed even London fog or blustery rain didn't put her off.

*They were surprised I didn't complain about the cold or the wet. I liked the rain.*

On Sundays, after a period of sermon-tasting among many of the larger congregations of London, she settled at Westminster Chapel. Gazing down from the dizzying height of the Chapel's upper gallery, she listened intently, along with two thousand others, to the lilting Welsh tones of Dr Martyn Lloyd-Jones. But after two years she'd had enough!

*The Doctor got far too deeply into Predestination in the end!*

Unlike her sister Lydia, now engaged in missionary work in Lebanon, Amal had never been to a Bible college. If she had thought about it at all in her early years, when one role after another seemed to demand her immediate attention, it did not seem to matter. But now, as something of a missionary calling was beckoning, it presented as a definite lack. It was also not lost on her that others on her course felt similarly called; but they all seemed to have attended Bible college – many had been to the Salvation Army's own Training College.

So Amal pursued another option – she signed up for evening classes at the London Bible College situated in Marylebone Road.

*(The Planetarium was right opposite!)*

The Bible had always been infinitely precious to Amal. She still loved to plumb its depths, while recognising there was always so much more to learn. She attended classes twice weekly – but sadly had to give up before the end of the course as midwifery studies took inevitable precedence.

But during each of the two summers she arranged her annual leave to coincide with the Keswick Convention – a long-established Christian gathering, part holiday, part conference. The busy resort of Keswick, cradled between the crags and fells of the northern Lake District, and looking out over Derwent Water, is ideal for such a gathering, with its wide choice of accommodation. And the main meetings are held in a five-thousand seater tent.

'Keswick' had already been going for ninety summers when Amal attended; other conferences might have had a missionary emphasis – perhaps with fringe meetings or a book-table – but Keswick made missionary work centre-stage. In its early days a link had been identified between individual spiritual renewal, or 'holiness', and consecration to a specific lifetime's work. As a result many responded to a Godly prompting to work overseas. There were speakers from around the world, and it also became a gathering place for those home on leave or retired from the 'field'. One such was a Miss Beare, who to Amal's endless fascination had worked amongst Arabs in Jerusalem. When once Amal discovered she lived in Hackney, this hospitable ex-missionary, who happened to have a unique way with baked potatoes, soon found her fireside in her little flat had an irresistible pull for a succession of students from the nearby Mothers'.

The money Amal had saved while working in Saudi stretched well beyond day-to-day expenses and two visits to the Lake District: she was left with enough for a 'proper' holiday. It would be a long time before such an opportunity occurred again, so with one of her Canadian friends she planned a fifteen-day 'trip of a lifetime' to Switzerland. Neither of them had seen anything of mainland Europe; when it came to it even the ferry trip was exciting, with the White Cliffs receding, and Calais drawing into sight. But alas this was as far as they got. They both discovered, too late, they needed visas! There was a somewhat less exciting return trip to Dover, where they stayed overnight, settling for a very pleasant two weeks in Scotland instead.

Another favourite place for an occasional break was the farm in Suffolk which belonged to a cousin of Pauline Stammers. Suddon Hall, near Debenham, was both grand and extensive.

*It was like a moated castle – it used to belong to a lord.*

Many of the farms in the area were at least semi-moated. Suddon Hall's 'moat' was in reality a large pond, but the important thing is it was big enough for Pauline's cousin's six children to launch a boat. Both parents and children loved to share their rambling home with returning friends from around the world, particularly missionaries. It was a working farm, mainly arable – cereals and sugar beet – but with a cow for milk, and also a donkey. Amal was in her element, laughing with the children as she told stories from her own childhood farmyard memories.

In the summer of 1965, all exams passed, and the required number of supervised deliveries, both in the hospital and on the district, duly completed, it was time for Amal to depart.

She was returning briefly to Syria – but she had already had another significant encounter which not only confirmed her call to work in the Middle East, but indicated a possible role in an area of the Gulf with which she was as yet unfamiliar, but where she would spend the rest of her working life.

...She walked through the archway between these buildings
(This is the same building today, but no longer housing the
Mothers' Hospital)

…comparatively remote and more primitive community

# Chapter Ten
## *Ras al Khaimah*

The 'significant encounter' in London was with Helen Fearnow, an American midwifery student a year ahead of Amal; Helen and her husband were now settled back in the Trucial States region of the Gulf. But now in her parents' home in *Al Kafroun* again, Amal had temporarily forgotten about Helen; she was anxiously seeking guidance once more as to where she would eventually settle down. She set off to another Bible conference – this time in the cool mountains of Lebanon.

*Ain Zhalta* was a favoured resort for expatriates working throughout the Gulf region. Oil had yet to make its impact, electricity remained unreliable, if available at all, and 'air-con' unheard of, so a summer spent high up in Lebanon's *Ain Zhalta,* where the air smells pine-sweet and water flows freely, made the rest of the year back in the desert just bearable. It was an ideal place for Christian retreats and Bible conferences. Unknown to Amal, Helen was there with her family from *Ras al Khaimah*, one of the Trucial States – so Amal and Helen met again. It was as if God was not letting her escape.

*In London Helen and I had never exchanged addresses.*
*I had gone straight back to Syria.*

Helen and Glenn Fearnow were both nurses, and had already been working longterm in various parts of the Middle East; Helen, now a midwife, had opened a midwifery clinic in *Ras al Khaimah,* or RAK as it was colloquially known.

This time Helen and Amal recognised something of a mutual commitment, a joint passion for helping particularly women of the remote desert regions – and without further hesitation Amal signed a contract to work with her for two years.

In 1971 the British protectorate of the Trucial States would become the United Arab Emirates, a grouping of seven sheikhdoms or emirates. Very unequal in size, status, and eventual wealth, in each case the name of the Emirate is the same as its principal city. Abu Dhabi and Dubai are now internationally known – but RAK is one of the smaller northern Emirates, remaining considerably less wealthy. In 1965, when Amal was settling in to RAK, there were only two other Christian expatriate medical centres throughout the Emirates: the Sarah Hosman Hospital in Sharjah, founded way back in 1951, and the American Hospital founded 1960 in *Al Ain*, an oasis town in the remote eastern border region of Abu Dhabi.

So Amal joined Helen straight away. She flew from Syria into RAF Sharjah. Before the oil brought its international prestige, particularly to Abu Dhabi and Dubai, the RAF base at Sharjah provided the only airport. The British Army was also there, and among the officers was a Major John Pott, a keen Christian who made a point of welcoming any new Christian worker to the region, knowing how little was established at that time. He arranged the ongoing transport for many a bewildered arrival; in Amal's case he drove her all the way to RAK. There was no road, and the simplest way was to drive along the shore for an hour or so, north from Sharjah, when the tide was out.

*In fact the journey was shorter in those days; the inland road they eventually built was crooked.*

A year later this well-respected military man was due to retire; he hired a *dhow,* a traditional coastal vessel, on which to hold his generous farewell party. By this time Amal was well immersed within the Christian expatriate community, so was very much part of this significant and heart-warming event. The Major arranged for his mess staff to wait on everyone; there was an abundance of food, including rare ice-cream, and everyone agreed afterwards they had been treated like royalty, as they sailed sedately up and down the Dubai creek to the accompaniment of the on-board military band.

Helen's clinic was fully equipped to Western standards, including of course a well-appointed delivery room with adaptable couch. But many of the women, having been accustomed to simply squatting in the sand for their babies to be born, favoured the floor for their delivery.

After delivery the women could stay for five days. Helen and Amal had prepared a five-day low-key programme of Bible lessons: they made sure the basics were all covered in five days!

Sarah Hosman was right. To Amal's delight there seemed to be no barrier to speaking to women about the Gospel. Indeed particularly among the men there was often an open-mindedness and enthusiasm for debate. At that time Islamic militancy was unheard of, the hubris of oil discovery had yet to develop, and the subsequent resistant attitudes and fears not encountered – at least, not within the city.

*Many women believed – but didn't stay believing when they returned home. Having had forbidden contact with Christians, they returned to family life ruled by their husband.*

There were other lessons Amal soon learnt – so very different from anything encountered in London.

Very soon she became acquainted with the devastating effects of female circumcision – or FGM as it is now known. This had been new to Helen; it was not something Amal had previously encountered either: back in her homeland it was not practised among any of the various communities. But as with many things which directly impacted her professionally, she soon became an expert in the subject; arming herself with plain facts – and a few scare stories –

she was soon able to hold forth in the strongest of terms concerning the unmitigated disastrous results of FGM, advising her patients of the emotional and physical damage they would be inflicting on their daughters, should they choose to continue the practice.

As if that were not enough, there were other obstetric hazards for women in that region of the Gulf. After a first delivery the traditional desert practice was for the woman to pack salt into the birth canal, in order, as it was understood, to prevent bleeding and infection. But it also caused desiccation and shrinking of the birth canal. Subsequent deliveries were fraught with danger. Dr Hosman however had managed to devise a solution, a series of incisions which enabled the birth to take place without resorting to Caesarean sections – which for isolated clinics were out of the question.

During her second year with Helen a woman came from a town called *Sha'am*, situated even further up the Emirates coast, about as far as you can go before the border with Oman – for the delivery of her eighth child. All her previous babies had died. A woman would not normally consider coming all that way, but she and her husband were desperate – maybe the clinic could save this one. Helen and Amal each had their own caseload; this was one of Amal's, and she took the decision to give the baby (– an extra precious baby boy) a course of penicillin injections, in case the problem all along had been syphilis. It seemed to be the right treatment: with much praise to God the new little family returned to Sha'am.

*We went back to Sha'am to visit her. Both the woman and her mother became believers.*

The inhabitants of a small town such as Sha'am were generally poorer than the people of the city of RAK. Amal eagerly anticipated her first visit to one of their homes. As she stepped over the threshold, she whispered a prayer of gratitude for the privilege, and also of blessing on the household.

'Come and see your baby!' the mother cried excitedly, as soon as she saw Amal. The baby's basket-weave cradle was hanging from the ceiling; a layer of sand covered the bottom of the cradle as an excellent and disposable substitute to the baby having to wear a nappy. The homes were simpler here – somehow closer to the desert. Many slept on the ground outside, with goats and chickens all around.

Later Amal felt the newly confessed faith had evaporated somewhat with the baby's mother – but not so with the grandmother. Amal continued to visit, forging a link particularly with the grandmother, and giving her a New Testament.

But then gradually Amal started to be aware of something strange – a new and unsettling sensation began to intrude on her quiet acceptance of her current location and fulfilling role. It seemed as if Sha'am was calling her; every time she returned from there, she felt she was leaving a little bit of her heart behind.

She was coming to the end of her initial two-year commitment to Helen. Could she, she wondered, develop her own clinic in Sha'am. But how on earth could she, a single woman, live alone in that comparatively remote and more primitive community? – a community on the very edge of a newly emerging nation with among other things only 9,000 phones to its name (none of which were likely to be found in Sha'am). She decided to go home and talk to her seventy-seven-year-old father. Amal was about to be very persuasive.

...a massive flag painted on the side of the mountain

# Chapter Eleven

## *The Tent*

Rain poured off the rocky mountain tops and swept through hidden gulleys onto the stony desert below. Streets not built to cope were awash, and tufts of grass and long-forgotten desert blooms began to appear. In the closing months of 1967 Amal and her father had arrived in Sha'am in the midst of a rare desert rainstorm.

Her persuasive powers had won, and Antonius had agreed to accompany his daughter, and help her settle into her new home. They lodged temporarily with a friend – and along with everyone else, in the week-long rainstorm, which the old stone houses with their wooden lintels were not built to withstand, they experienced the ruin of some of their yet-unpacked belongings. Most dwellings in Sha'am are much more geared to the open-air life – a palm-branch roof over the lean-to, with furniture, including soft furnishings, underneath. Here the household can sit out in the shade to catch any available sea-breeze. They just do not expect it to rain.

When the rain had finished, then came the malaria; Amal was hit by another bout. She resented being laid low when everything within her wanted to throw herself into the work.

*Once again I called out to God to save me; it would not be good for his name if I die here and now – not good for a daughter of his.*

Recovery came more quickly this time than when she had been hospitalised as a child.

At nearly forty, Amal felt a lifetime had passed; for years she had been drawing ever nearer to what she believed would be her goal, but not quite getting there. She looked back at her time in Gaza, then the Golan Heights: how deeply joyful she had felt, even in the poorest of places. Would that deep satisfaction be hers again – in this place? Through all the years of preparation she never lost her focus, her sense of having an ultimate calling – now this was surely it. The little coastal town of Sha'am, in the Emirate of *Ras al Khaimah,* did indeed become her home, for fifty years.

Far from being a pretty place, and devoid of much traditional desert 'charm', the town nevertheless held at least one natural advantage as far as Amal was concerned: the sea was barely three minutes' walk away. Amal wondered if she could ever now live for long without the sea. Until well into old age she continued to enjoy swimming, more often than not at sunset – and invariably fully clothed.

Sitting at the extreme tip of the 'toe' of the Arabian Peninsula, Sha'am looks out across the busy and strategic Straits of Hormuz; for its hinterland it has the barren Hajar Mountains – and just the other side of those mountains lies the Sultanate of Oman. This makes Sha'am very much a border town, and as with many border communities, the national flag takes on particular importance: when once the UAE was founded, four years after Amal arrived, the Emirati flag went up all over Sha'am – including a massive flag painted on the side of the mountain. Its permanent visibility was assured by the herds of black goats and the wild donkeys who kept the thorn bushes well cropped back.

Sha'am was originally a sardine-fishing and pearl-diving village; now a massive limestone quarry and five cement factories line the road into RAK. This was potentially the one good road, constructed soon after Amal's arrival – but quickly rutted and ruined by the huge cement lorries going back and forth, supplying material with which to construct the promenades along the water-fronts of the more opulent Sharjah, Dubai and Abu Dhabi, many miles to the south.

Amal's good relations with *Sheikh Saqr,* ruler of the RAK Emirate, were to be key to her ability to remain; and the relationship began almost straight away. She had to seek his permission to purchase a plot of land to start her work.

*'Who told you to work in Sha'am?' the Sheikh asked me.*
*I replied 'God has sent me, and you will give me a visa!'*

The Sheikh was only too aware of RAK's general lack of medical care at that time – and how much depended on outside support. He asked her if she would go beyond her midwifery sphere, and treat men as well as women. So for some years Amal was something of the local unofficial pharmacist. The Sheikh was both impressed and grateful; things were off on a good footing.

Amal then began to look around for suitable property, or land to purchase.

It was Helen Fearnow who first suggested the tent.

All through the devastating floods, followed by malaria, (all of which Amal dismissed as 'spiritual attack'), Helen had kept a caring eye on her. Aware of Amal's unfazed determination she gently put forward the suggestion of a tent: it could perhaps work as a possible 'stop-gap'. Throughout the desert regions of the Arabian Peninsula and the Middle East, no-one felt that far removed from tent-dwelling; tents were in fact still very much in use, and not just by the *Bedu*. Amal's own surname 'Boody' was a derivative of 'Bedouin'. Never yet having settled permanently in one place, the nomadic concept was still very much part of Amal's make-up; she thought the tent was a wonderful idea!

Their first purchase was in a style more military than Bedouin; it was khaki-coloured, but rather small. The potential was clear, however, and she sent off for a much larger tent – which had to come all the way from Ireland. But for that first year the small tent doubled as Amal's clinic, and their first home.

As a midwife Amal was a novelty in the area, and pregnant women started turning up almost straight away. Cautious at first, but having little medical alternative, they were soon won over by the perceived impression Amal was one of them – similar in dress, complexion and language, if not in dialect and headcovering; they coped with her assertive no-nonsense professional approach, softened by her eye-twinkling humour – and they wondered, half envious, at the fact she had no husband to tell her what to do. Gradually they came to trust her. Not wishing to lose momentum Amal very soon started a Sunday school for children.

Antonius was in all probability more respected initially than Amal. The presence of an older male guardian with white hair provided her with just the respectability and status she needed. A dapper gentleman with a kindly personality and a taste for a smart suit, Antonius was companionable for Amal, and clearly proud of his one unmarried daughter.

*Every morning when he stepped out of the tent and caught sight of the mountains, my father said 'Glory to God!'*

But eventually she did have to cope on her own, as her ageing father had to return permanently to Syria, to be with Amal's equally elderly mother. By this time the much larger tent had arrived.

So Amal's new 'Maternity Unit' consisted of a large rectangular tent divided into two by a curtain. One side was the 'delivery suite', the other, her private quarters.

When a woman was in labour she would move into the unit with a female relative who looked after her non-medical needs. Amal would examine the patient and regularly check on her. She had some freedom to speak directly to the women on matters of faith – but in her forthright way this often did not seem enough. So additionally she often let them hear her praying for them. She went into the other half of the tent which was her private space, and here prayed loudly and fervently for the woman in labour, and for her family.

The ladies usually stayed with her for one or two days post-delivery, before going home. Their companion would cook their food during this time.

A small charge was levied, which Amal increased somewhat reluctantly over the years. The coveted iron tablets seemed to be prized almost as much as the baby, as their take-home reward.

Amal's sensitive and spiritualised construct meant at times she was particularly vulnerable living on her own – especially in a tent. There were incidents, such as the night a thief came, which would have been too much for some – but they just seemed to strengthen her resolve.

*There were noises at night. I felt someone didn't want me to be there. Sha'am seemed like the centre of the devil's kingdom.*

For one period she had a large cockerel which strutted round with all the supposed arrogance of the males of his species; Amal's childhood experience with animals was such that she had complete control over the handsome bird – and it could be relied on to run after any children who came to make fun of her, or to bother her in her tent. The cockerel had to keep the goats at bay also; they disappeared up the mountain sides during the day, chewing at the *ghaf* trees and scrubby thorn bushes as they went, but come evening they would return to the homes of their owners – ever hungry, and on the lookout for something different to eat! They were certainly known for eating anything, with paper money seeming to be a particular delicacy, so again a tent-dweller would have to be on their guard. All was not lost however, if a precious item did disappear – as long as you knew immediately which goat was the culprit. It would simply be slaughtered by the owner, in anticipation of the evening meal, the foreign object being retrieved from the goat's stomach as part of the preparation process.

But one day alas, a young boy managed to grab hold of Amal's cockerel, and killed it, hanging it up at the entrance to her tent.

Amal's love for children won through: she felt sorry for the boy, and decided she needed to pray for him; she wanted to be sure to say the right thing if she ever caught sight of the boy again. When this did happen, however, she suddenly forgot her good intentions – and grabbed the nearest big stick!

*Suddenly I remembered, dropped the stick, and ran back to my bedside; I told the Lord how sorry I was, and asked him to forgive me!*

One very practical solution to possible loneliness and vulnerability was Amal's love of hospitality. As well as amongst the desert women, she was becoming increasingly well-known among the expatriate Christian workers in the other cities of the Emirates. She had already earned the distinction of being the first Middle Easterner ever to go as a full-time Christian worker to the Gulf region. Word soon spread, like wildfire some said, that this lone Syrian lady loved to have visitors – and especially families with children. So often one or other of these families would come and stay in the school holidays. Amal bedded down as many as she could within the tent; dads and older boys slept outside.

She served them sumptuous meals of goat, lamb or salted fish, on a bed of rice, and with plenty of fresh vegetables. Huge plates of dates and other fresh fruit came out for dessert. They were amazed at what she could produce with the most primitive of cooking facilities.

There was no fresh cow's milk, and camel milk was only available if you owned a camel. But that did not stop Amal providing her visitors with quantities of memorable yoghurt made using powdered milk. Later the repertoire was extended further when tinned fruit started to appear in the local souk. Water was initially drawn from a well and sold to her in goat skin containers by a man with a donkey, or by a lady who (of course) carried the container on her head.

The most difficult thing was the heat. For Amal's first four years she had no electricity – a state of affairs which she shared with the occupants of all but the most sumptuous Sha'am dwellings. Air-conditioning was anyway hardly known at that time, and every summer many expatriate workers headed home, leaving the steamy Gulf Coast behind, where the three summer months were known anecdotally as the hundred days of hell! Amal too tended to travel then, taking the opportunity to go home to family in Syria, or friends in Beirut, both of which places were infinitely cooler in comparison. Sometimes she had somewhere specific to go – there were the summer conferences in *Ain Zhalta* in the mountains of Lebanon, and once she went to India to stay with some Indian colleagues she had met in RAK.

When electricity did start to arrive, so did television! Amal rejected any thought of this latest incarnation of decadence, noticing how it was taking over from other forms of hospitality, as those who could afford this newest form of entertainment had to cope with a stream of visitors who could not!

Towards the end of her time in the tent, Amal received some visitors from the hospital in *Al Ain*, the oasis town in the midst of hundreds of miles of sandy desert in the Emirate of Abu Dhabi – and several hours' journey from Abu Dhabi city. An Australian friend of hers had arranged to bring a group of four midwifery colleagues to meet Amal, and to learn of her unique challenges and struggles, whilst also enjoying her Bedouin-like hospitality. In return they invited Amal to stay in *Al Ain*; its situation inland meant the heat was dryer and more bearable than the cloying damp heat of the coastal areas. In fact *Al Ain* was something of a resort for Emiratis and Westerners alike. Here there were gardens to enjoy, providing a riot of colour and scent among the shady date palms, and cooled and watered by the ancient system of channels running underground from the oasis. Fountains played in the parks, keeping the grass green, and the pink and white oleander bushes fragrant. Even today *Al Ain* is still considered to be a beautiful city, with high-rises, apart from the Hilton, strictly not allowed. Amal was delighted to add this to her list of places to visit to escape the summer furnace of the coast.

But one of her most significant summer excursions was in the July of 1974, when she received an invitation to attend the first Lausanne Congress. She had been invited, along with 2,700 other delegates, to attend this international gathering convened by Dr Billy Graham, and to be held in the enormous conference centre on the shores of Lake Geneva, Switzerland. The purpose was to address the challenges of the global spread of Christianity, particularly from the traditional 'Christian' West, to the nations of Africa, Asia and South America. Ever since her failed 'trip of a lifetime' which should have taken place at the end of her stay in London, Amal had cherished the possibility that one day she would have a second chance to see the gleaming spires and onion-domes of mediaeval Europe. The conference was exciting in its way – but Lausanne's cobbled streets and Gothic cathedral fulfilled yet another dimension of Amal's endlessly roving and adventurous spirit.

She returned to the desert with a renewed sense of calling. She was more convinced than ever that this was indeed the place where she was meant to be. For the first time in her life, and ironically in a tent, that potent Arab symbol of impermanence and transition, Amal was planning to stay put. Now she needed a more permanent dwelling.

# Chapter Twelve

## *'The Richness of Remaining'*

The tent had served as home, office, clinic and labour ward for almost ten years now, and there were times when Amal might have up to three patients 'on the go' at once. She desperately needed a more durable property, and she decided the easiest thing, at least in the short term, would be to take up an offer she had received some time previously of two container units; she could live in one, and the other could be her maternity department. The fact that no-one else in Sha'am had ever lived in a container home, or for that matter even seen one, bothered her not one bit. In fact it reminded her of how the Palestinian refugees had lived in the camp at the foot of the Golan Heights – her time with them, the exhausting work, the sights, the smells, all now etched golden in her memory.

The land on which she had the tent was already hers. Always someone of modest requirements, Amal anticipated much of her day-to-day living would still take place outside; with this in mind, between the two containers she constructed a palm branch shelter, a variation on the cool and traditional *barasti,* so favoured throughout the Gulf region; the inevitable row of little onlookers could not believe their eyes when the containers arrived – but were reassured as the familiar *barasti* took shape.

Meanwhile an occasional shift in Amal's work pattern eased both her potential loneliness, and pressure on her premises: some of her work began to be increasingly based 'on the district'.

When Amal first arrived in Sha'am there were still only two Land Rovers throughout the entire local population –

and she drove one of them. This type of vehicle was invaluable in the southern more populated areas of the UAE, being generally ideal for the sandy territory. Driving on desert or on the beach the tyres would be let down: like camels' feet they coped better when splayed.

But Amal's local desert was of the stony variety, and the roads and tracks consequently less forgiving. More and more she was driving inland, over the roughest of terrain. On one occasion she found herself rushing out to help a woman in obstructed labour; as so often happened, the mother had left it almost too late to obtain help. With limited equipment Amal struggled to do what she could – the baby was in an impossible 'lie', and had been stuck for three days; maternal and foetal distress were both setting in. In the end the baby was delivered, but did not draw breath straight away. He survived, but to Amal's great grief, he later appeared to be brain-damaged. As well as feeling severely under-equipped in these situations, although surrounded by the village people she loved, Amal felt perversely very alone.

So what did she do for obstetric back-up? Exactly how far was it to the nearest suitably qualified doctor? When Amal first arrived there was no doctor in the whole of RAK. If difficulties presented themselves within the tent (and if there were enough time, and transport were available), Amal would send the woman with a letter to the Maktoum Hospital in Dubai – a journey which could take two hours. Later in the 1970s a doctor came to RAK, and by the 1980s gleaming new hospitals were starting to be built – so Amal referred patients there.

Then one day the call came from a village even higher up in the mountains. Here the tracks are unsuitable even for Land Rovers – she would have to walk.

High up on the summit of the mountains there is a plateau area where the air is cooler, and where crops can therefore be grown. So there amongst the ancient ruins of the hilltop forts a newer community was able to develop. Amal would never have been able to find her way up the steep and winding mountain path, but the woman who brought the urgent message waited for her, then guided her back across the mountains – a walk of three or four hours. She returned to the mountain top community on two or three more occasions, sometimes staying overnight; someone always came to fetch her, waiting until Amal had made up a bed roll to take with her. Her guide would then carry it on her head, whilst at the same time negotiating the steep and narrow paths.

Throughout the 70s, and on into the 80s and 90s, Amal's western Christian friends from across the Emirates continued to come and stay. Generally they camped in the grounds of her compound, as opposed to within her container home, where space was at a premium. They came for the fun and relaxation, whilst also appreciating her more serious side; she had such a straight-forward way with spiritual insights, which some hoped would rub off on their restless adolescent offspring. She could be remarkably blunt if she learnt they were not currently attending church!

But for younger children it was regarded as a camping holiday at the seaside. If she were free, Amal would join them for their early mornings or late afternoons on the beach.

For as long as anyone could remember, both the beach and the sea had been used as a toilet by the locals. (The time-honoured question posed by all health workers everywhere was re-phrased here as 'Have you visited the beach yet today?') This was a hazard sea-bathing Westerners simply became used to. But after Amal's container home had been in situ for a couple of years, good news arrived: Sha'am was being plumbed in! Some older residents inevitably took time to adapt, but Amal went ahead and purchased a third container to house a bathroom. Things gradually improved on the beach, and swimmers now had only to acclimatise themselves to the periodic invasions of jelly-fish.

Picnicking in the desert was also a favourite occupation. As Gulf Arabs traditionally sit on the floor, it was never any effort, even for the oldest of the party, to take their place on the blanket – where a plastic tablecloth would then be spread out in the middle. Amal enjoyed joining both Arab and Western friends on these occasions. She also loved trips out to the *wadis*. These dramatic geographical features were common throughout the mountainous areas of RAK; some were cut so deeply into the rocky landscape that the tops of their abundant palm tree foliage were barely visible at ground level. Little excuse was needed by any Arab family to enjoy these kinds of leisure activities; they love their desert, and Amal too felt the desert was part of her.

Another treat, as far as Amal was concerned, was to spend a day in Fujairah, across on the other side of the peninsula (which juts up into the Straits of Hormuz).

Here, on the eastern coast of the UAE, another maternity hospital had been founded, at about the same time as Amal started her work in Sha'am. It was run by an international team of Christian midwives and other female health workers. They too were very hospitable, taking a great interest in anyone whom God sent their way. They became firm friends of Amal. Here she enjoyed the opportunity to chat through some of the challenges of remote midwifery, whilst being relieved of some of her gnawing loneliness. But she also found Fujairah to be the place where she realised her uncompromising temperament might not fit in so well as part of a multi-national team of (equally) strong-minded women. God knew what he was doing, in placing her on her own within a local community.

It only took a few years for Amal's 'garden' area to look well established, with one or two trees, and a protective hedge to give her and her patients some privacy. But sadly, in 1983 the local authorities planned to build a road along a route which would encroach on her land.

*This was intentional; the authorities wanted to give me a hard time.*

In fact most of the time the authorities demonstrated respect for Amal. Back in the time of the tent, when asked what they thought of her work, the local sheikh had replied 'She is the mercy of God to us.' But with Amal's strong opinions, and the constant commercial and ideological pressures of local government, the relationship was always going to have its highs and lows.

In order to build their new road, the authorities needed to requisition some of her land. They paid her modestly in compensation, enabling her to buy some property in RAK city, which after a while she was able to sell. Even so, when they eventually started building the threatened road, Amal was not going to be a pushover.

*I went and sat on one of their piles of earth – I was determined to stop them going any further.*

She did not prevail of course – but she continued treading the fine line between constantly having to take her stand, as she saw it, and often on her own, while on the other hand keeping in with the Sheikh.

Meanwhile, her outdoor extended living area was developing apace. Over the years it gradually became a second kitchen area, a seating area, even a washing area (with a Heath-Robinson-type shower unit rigged up behind one of the containers).

In one of the remaining *ghaf* trees Amal installed a beehive, with the idea of producing honey; she was a great believer in honey as a source of immediate energy in labour. But then, once again, it attracted the attentions of a thief. At around two o'clock one morning she suddenly found she was wide awake, listening to a noise in the garden. She went out to have a look – and there was the thief, half way up the tree where the beehive was, cutting thorny branches off as he went up.

*So I thought I'd let him clear the way for me to get the honey. But he was scared when he saw me – I was all in white!*

Scared stiff by this apparition – in reality Amal draped in a white nightdress – the thief ran away.

In another corner of her plot she installed an enormous dove cot. But this was not out of any aesthetic desire to share her garden with pretty white doves. She had previously found two baby pigeons which she nurtured into full growth; they had given her an idea, and they, or perhaps just subsequent inhabitants of the cot, proved to be ideal sources of additional protein for her and her visitors.

When the final dimensions of her property were established, Amal placed a wire fence on the outer perimeter, outside the thorny hedge, to give protection as much as possible from the munching by the skinny cows who roamed the town, as well as by the omnivorous goats.

Not a great cultivator, she nevertheless knew a thing or two about weeds, and whether on her own patch or someone else's could confidently identify the edible ones. She could spot them too in the public parks, increasingly a feature of town planning in the UAE. Whether alone or walking with friends, she was shameless in her enthusiasm for bringing home huge quantities in one go; they looked nothing special, but soaked, washed, boiled and cooled, and chopped with tomatoes and onions from the souk, they would be transformed into a most remarkable salad.

One day a lady was brought to Amal in terrible pain. She had been expecting twins, and the first baby was already born. The second however was in a 'transverse lie' – a position virtually incompatible with normal delivery. Amal had previously told her to attend the hospital for the birth, but her labour pains, so the patient claimed, had not given her enough time to get there. It was always annoying to Amal that when she did transfer such patients, the hospital staff would give her a hard time for taking on such cases herself, instead of referring them to the hospital. *They didn't seem to understand that the women just turned up!*

The doctor delivered the baby, but did not clear the airway, and since the baby was blue and had not breathed, he declared that the baby was dead! The doctor gave him to the mother who accepted what she was told, and held him on her lap. Meanwhile, Amal had been watching, and decided to pray fervently. Suddenly, the baby started crying: her prayers had been answered!

Observing the two boys growing up, she could not help looking out for any signs of brain damage. She gradually came to realise that no such signs were appearing – finally watching them disappear off to university!

The experience of many of the Christian expatriate workers underlined the fact that many Emiratis, particularly the isolated desert dwellers, or the hardy *Bedu* with their camel stock and rich and colourful culture, or just the poorer and less well educated, all appreciated being prayed for, when their new Christian friends came to visit. In fact it was almost an expectation from these 'people of the Book', as Christians were labelled, and was not perceived as a threat to their own Islamic faith. In addition, being traditionally a non-literate society, they loved story-telling – and Amal had stories in abundance. She had a way of telling Bible stories that made them sound as if they had just happened yesterday.

These more remote people, the communities most out of touch with the Gulf's headlong rush into modernity, were the very people Amal loved.

And it was certainly boom time in the Emirates. Since the discovery of oil, skyscrapers and modern roads were appearing almost overnight; electricity stations and other plant were urgently needed. Soon workers from other parts of Asia had to be allowed in to do the lion's share of the newly available manual labour. For the first time government-built housing started to appear; moreover Emiratis began to find themselves wealthier, and started to abandon their traditional coral block or stone homes for grander designs – Afghan and Indian workers and their families were only too pleased to take over these humbler dwellings.

So Amal's clientele changed also, as she continued to feel happiest among the poor – and this inevitably included a proportion of the immigrant population. In Sha'am a whole new community of colourful Baluchis from Pakistan were soon arriving with their families.

At the same time Amal was increasingly a favoured guest in the homes of the local Emiratis whom she'd known for so long. Sitting only with the women and children, their dwellings being generally segregated, she found she was entertained with the most intimate and gossipy details of their lives; they in turn loved her down-to-earth sense of humour, as she relaxed and laughed with them at their children's increasingly fractious antics as the evenings wore on.

Gradually there came a new development: she began to be invited to the weddings of 'her' babies; soon she was delivering the second generation.

...ideal sources of additional protein

...the ancient ruins of the hilltop forts

Picnicking in the desert...a favourite occupation

...gleaming new hospitals were starting to be built (Sha'am Hospital today)

# Chapter Thirteen

## *World Traveller*

By 1997 Amal had been in Sha'am for thirty years. At sixty-seven it was time for her to retire: handing in her notice to the UAE's Ministry of Health, she delivered her final baby that same year.

Now there would be time to indulge further her two great pleasures in life – entertaining, and being entertained. She continued to be welcomed into the homes of local friends, with a unique mixture of sisterly familiarity on the one hand, and adulation fit for royalty on the other. She had more time too to visit friends back in the city of *Ras al Khaimah*. The Fearnows had left, but other western expatriates, or 'expats' as they were increasingly known, seemed constantly to be arriving. New churches were springing up, strictly for expats only of course, as it would be anathema for an Emirati to be anything but Muslim. There were English-medium Anglican and Baptist churches for the westerners, Catholic and other churches for the Indians, Pentecostal churches for the burgeoning Filipino community – and there were the Arabic-speaking churches for Middle-Easterners, of which the Egyptian Copts were the largest in number.

When Amal was in town she favoured the English-speaking churches.

*The Egyptian churches spoke the wrong Arabic!*

Many of the denominations shared premises, meeting at different times. The expats, from professional to labouring, were now beginning to be the majority of the population – and Indians were the majority of those.

Amal also attended Bible study groups, many held in homes. As ever, new acquaintances quickly became her friends; the children of those in the groups still remember her as the 'lady with the smile and the long black dress'. She was in fact gradually adapting her own style of attire – some said it was neither one thing nor the other: not Western, which was mostly the style of her youth, nor that of the heavily draped Gulf Arab women among whom she lived. Since arriving in Sha'am she had always bought the long kaftans readily available from the souks – choosing bright colours in the early days, she now seemed to favour black.

She had a reputation for preferences in other areas also. In characteristic style she did not hold back on her intense dislike of modern forms of worship – especially the songs; if challenged she would happily give a satirical rendering to prove her point.

The city of RAK, although still small compared with Dubai, was changing also. The telecom tower, a shiny blue glass building with a giant white golf ball on the top, was the first prominent modern building – and it still stands out today.

The borders of the city constantly expanded with the development of the Emiratis' large and increasingly luxurious homes. Most of the professional expat community, Asians, Americans, or Europeans, lived in modern gated compounds of less ostentatious housing, each consisting of about thirty homes. (These new-builds frequently sported the bright blue or green fashionable pantiles on the roof; Amal could not resist commenting on how much their wavy effect reminded her of peristalsis!) She was as relaxed visiting in these, or in the plush Emirati homes, as she was in the poorer communities who were being left behind.

Most of the gated compounds had their own swimming pool. The professional expats were into water-sports in a big way. Among the local wealthy Emiratis, however, camel-racing was the latest craze.

The souk was still at the heart of things – but was considered inferior to that of Sharjah, Dubai or Abu Dhabi. A cinema was opened when the big shopping mall was built

– at about the same time as the Hilton, with all its attendant international expectations, arrived in town. Since her arrival in 1965 Amal had been witness to the incredible effect of the oil boom on the United Arab Emirates – and to the parallel changes in the city of RAK, which always remained stoically a few paces behind the Gulf region as a whole.

Amal's longer distance travelling continued apace also. She was able to spend more time in Syria (as well as having first one nephew then another come and stay with her). Her homeland was now very different: her parents had both died, in their nineties, and in 2002 then 2006 she lost first one sister then another, Amal returning home in each case to look after them. The farm was inevitably different also, being modernised under her brothers' management – and under the Assads the country was changing fast.

In the hot season she travelled furthest, including return visits to friends in the UK – particularly to see Pauline, and to visit the farm in Suffolk, where the six children were now all grown up.

She still loved to visit around her expat friends within the UAE. Although retired professionally she still had strength and resilience, and would if necessary roll up her sleeves in any home she was visiting, and do whatever needed doing. According to some she had the ability to turn up on doorsteps at the most critical moments – 'as if sent by an angel' one close friend said. She could take over the running of an entire household – after the birth of the latest baby for instance.

She was known to sometimes bring, as her contribution to catering, a couple of frozen pigeons – a gift that was not always greeted with excitement. Her choice of meat staple was a source of fascination to many, particularly those visiting from the West. On one occasion, finding herself in the company of some expat scientists, she seized her opportunity to ask about something which was worrying her: sometimes her pigeons seemed to develop neck problems; their heads would get stuck in the wrong direction. This was greeted by dismissive hilarity from those who knew her well. But one veterinary surgeon, newly arrived to work in the Sheikh's camel laboratories, took her completely seriously – and everyone else by surprise: 'Oh that's Newcastle disease!' he immediately and uncompromisingly announced. The ever-resourceful Amal now had a poultry virus to cope with.

Amal was much in demand as an extra pair of hands at many a children's party, where she far outshone the best of professional story-tellers. Her repertoire was almost exclusively Bible stories – but her way of telling them gave them a unique and contemporary buzz. Inserting herself into the story at a vital moment, perhaps as the naughty lost sheep (called Amal), children and adults alike would be captivated.

She could now be absent from Sha'am for longer than before – sometimes two or three months at a time. Keeping as it were a nightdress under the pillow in countless homes across the Middle East and beyond, she nevertheless never changed how she felt about Sha'am.

*One of 'my' boys in RAK is now a local businessman;*
*he always gets my visa.*

Sha'am would always remain her home, the place to which she always wanted to return.

---------------------

Then, in the summer of 2018, while life was still demanding, and every moment full, Amal fell and fractured her femur.

Unusually she was spending June in RAK, and she was staying with friends.

Late one evening, walking round in the darkness of the less than familiar home, she suddenly missed her footing, and tripped over a step. Dazed and in obvious pain she struggled to get up unaided – but could not. No, she stated adamantly, she did not want an ambulance to come and fetch

100

her. Feeling desperately frustrated, her friends had no alternative for the time being but to make her comfortable with cushions where she was, and Amal, somewhat stubbornly it would seem, spent some hours on the unyielding tile floor. Eventually the severe pain drove her to relent, and she was taken to Saqr Hospital, the government hospital in RAK (named after Sheikh Saqr, who had granted her first visa).

The journey to the hospital was obviously traumatic for the patient; her uncompromising opinions were in danger of giving the ambulance team a rough ride also. First she did not want them to splint the leg, and then when they clearly had to, it was far too tight! She later claimed this gave her numbness in her leg for some months afterwards. Amal just was not in control for a change, and she did not know quite how to handle it.

Initially it was thought she had broken her hip, but x-rays showed a spiral fracture of her femur just below the hip. It took several tests and an excruciating journey to another hospital to determine if her heart was strong enough for the surgery. At her age they wanted to be sure.

*But I have a 'soldier heart'!*

They decided to go ahead; the operation would be essential if she were ever to walk again. Even so there was a fifty-fifty chance she would not survive. Amal, who lived her whole life in view of eternity, made up her mind this was her time to die, and was at peace.

The shock of waking up after the operation, and not in the immediate presence of her Heavenly Father, brought another round of fear-generated complaints.

*They put a rusty black metal plate in my leg that was the wrong size.*

Passive physiotherapy began almost straight away, gradually becoming more active, with a view to getting her

101

standing, then weight-bearing. Slowly strength and appetite returned, and Amal reluctantly learnt to use a walking frame.

Later in the summer she was moved to the new hospital at Sha'am – and to her delight she found she was in a room with a view of the sea. Her visitors moved her bed to be nearer the window. She looked out on the spangled ocean – 'her' ocean; it was calling to her, as it always did.

She received a constant stream of visitors, packing her room from dawn to dusk. As Amal held court, the staff wondered exactly who she was – some dignitary perhaps? Those who had travelled furthest naturally wished to stay a while; but they had to be prepared to be in and out of the room in shifts. Many visitors were local however; many Amal did not even know. They were all connected somehow to Sha'am and the babies she delivered. Some of them probably were the babies she delivered. The buzz, the laughter, and the constant attention, all lifted her spirits.

Sometimes she talked repetitively. Was she beginning to lose her memory? More likely she was simply repeating her stories for each fresh audience during the day. For most of the time she was alert and chatty, recounting the latest perceived medical incompetency with great relish.

Among those who loved her and were most immediately concerned with her well-being, thoughts began to turn to how she would manage when home. It did not seem likely that she would be able to live on her own again, certainly not in the immediate future, and certainly not back in her container home. There were steps to negotiate, and uneven ground, and generally hazards aplenty. In recent years she had tended to place outside her cabins the large items she no longer needed. Consequently the area around, in addition to the *al fresco* bathroom and kitchen areas, was an assault course of beds, cots and other furniture, superfluous wooden doors, the old delivery couch – and still the tent, now rolled up in a barrel, vermin-infested and disintegrating; the area was festooned with a myriad of electric cables, and prowled by the mutually respectful cats and pigeons.

Meanwhile the local rulers were keeping an eye on Amal. They wished to celebrate what she had done for them, and to honour her years of service. A broadcasting team turned up to interview her for a programme. Amal, as forthright as ever concerning her faith, took every opportunity to speak out. When she was asked about the most important thing in her life, they no doubt expected her to talk about her work, or her love of being in the UAE. Instead she simply shared the Gospel. One or two of the now elderly Christian midwives across in the Fujairah hospital had been honoured with citizenship for their long years of service; according to some, Amal's undiplomatic boldness cost her a similar privilege. Even in bed and in discomfort, she continued to be true to what she believed above everything else was her calling.

In fact decades on from her arrival in the Gulf, the spiritual atmosphere had shifted. Amal struggled with warnings she received from certain of the Sheikhs concerning the ease with which she was inclined to share her faith.

*What is this new Islam? I have never before been questioned about my faith.*

When it came to the vexed question of her long-term care, friends and relatives were putting off the moment of confrontation. For her part Amal would often broach the subject of her funeral perhaps, or her will, completely out of the blue, and with those least expecting it. Her relatives were often left out of the decision loop, receiving this information second hand, but they were grateful nevertheless for this great company of friends and supporters who cared for Amal with such love and respect.

Then in the November she fell and broke the other leg.

Once again she had surgery, and once again she made good progress, in spite of multiple challenges. This time round, the opportunity arose for her to convalesce in Al Ain – that fragrant oasis city which Amal had come to love – in the hospital where she had many friends.

By December she was doing really well once more, starting to walk with just one stick. She stayed in the nurses' accommodation, sharing the room of a very faithful friend.

But eventually arrangements had to be made for her to return to RAK; a flat had been rented for her to occupy for the next six months, with a live-in maid to care for her. Naturally when once she was moved back to RAK her thoughts turned to Sha'am: when would she be 'allowed' to live in her own home once again? She was taken to see it; it was obvious to friends that quantities of cleaning, clearing and sorting would need to be done before she could return, but it was also obvious Amal would not be put off forever! She brought the subject up, of her anticipated move back in, at fairly regular intervals.

But the flat was ideal for the time being, albeit a little further from the sea than she would have liked. Nothing daunted, Amal persuaded many of her visitors to drive her down to the beach. She still cherished a wish to swim again – or at the very least to get as much of herself as possible under the water. The tonic of being up to her neck in the sea was not something she would easily relinquish, even at this stage of her life.

But meanwhile some friends did come up with the ideal compromise: whenever Amal was taken out on an evening jaunt to the coast – and she confidently expected this to take place every day – a white plastic chair was taken along in the car also. It would be carried down to the beach, and into the sea, and there it was held in place in the lapping water. With support on both sides Amal would paddle out, floor-length skirts gathered to her knees – and there she would sit, Canute-like, with friends kicking and splashing in the water around her. Here she was relaxed and content. The fierceness went from the sun's rays, as it dropped over the horizon. She could feel the warm evening breeze on her face.

She laughed and joked with the friends around her, who loved her dearly: this suited Amal.

...the lady with the smile and the long black dress (Amal back in Sha'am in 2017)

…the spangled ocean...'her' ocean

# Postscript

Amal did return home!

In the spring of 2019, in the year in which she would be ninety, friends and relatives had run out of excuses: against expectation Amal was slowly regaining strength and agility, thereby gaining ground on her argument also. And anyway she continued to refuse to countenance any possible alternative to a return to her fragile and modest home, the place where she felt safest of all. All were amazed at her single-mindedness (not to say stubbornness) which appeared to strengthen in the face of the challenge, rather than weaken. Her supporters had no choice but to help her move back in, and there she remained, unfazed throughout the summer furnace. There was a storm too, with torrential rain and hail – not unlike her first summer in Sha'am. With the rain came high wind – but somehow the little dwelling, which was entirely without foundation, stood as steadfastly as the biblical house built on the rock.

Offers of a home elsewhere continued to come – but Amal withstood them with the same apparent fortitude possessed by her longsuffering cabins. Having amassed an array of walking-sticks and walking-frames, plus a wheelchair, and seeming to use each of them randomly, she continued to impress visiting friends with her strength of will and ability to care for herself, and to do what needed doing around the home.

Then, towards the end of the November of that year, the local Sheikh once again contacted her. Would she grant them the distinctive honour of accepting an award, for 'services to the region'? She accepted, on the condition she would not have to attend a reception; so the dignitaries agreed to come to her instead.

But she had not quite expected the celebrity status, however temporary, that accompanied the event.

From early morning on the day of the presentation, cars started parking outside her home. Photographers and local journalists walked up her path, and somewhat bemused, were squeezed into the cabin which comprised her tiny living area. When the Sheikh's entourage eventually arrived, the presentation, from the Sha'am Athletic and Cultural Club, went ahead. The award took the form of a large engraved plaque with her name on it; the citation was for 'her esteemed contribution to the region'. From a purely worldly point of view, this was recognition indeed, a well-deserved crowning of a lifetime's selfless devotion to others: the girl from the remote farming community of western Syria had earned her place in history, at least as far as Sheikh Saud bin Saqr, ruler of the Emirate of Ras al Khaimah, was concerned. As for Amal herself, she proved once again she was someone who could indeed, as Rudyard Kipling had put it, 'walk with Kings – nor lose the common touch'.

---------------------

Now we are approaching the end of 2020, and Amal has been grappling with a new concept – that of the Covid 19 virus. Gradually but alarmingly its effects have spread from country to country, right across the world. If Amal's band of carers ever thought they could shield her from an awareness of the growing concerns, the lockdowns and mask-wearing have now made it impossible. Over the months travel has become more and more limited, and Amal has had to face the fact she would not be seeing longer-distanced friends and relatives for a while. Her next-of kin live in Abu Dhabi, which has closed its borders to the other six Emirates, so they are unable to travel to RAK to see her. Keeping in touch with her by phone, they have been reassured she is in safe hands. Amal's own understanding of the situation waxes and wanes with her memory. One thing is sure, her propensity for espousing the latest conspiracy theory is as alive as ever: she is determined she does not need the vaccine. As one of her relatives says, 'She is the most resourceful and fiercely independent woman I have ever met.'

It has recently been decided Amal should move back to the apartment where she stayed before. Here she has help close at hand, plus the team of friends who keep in touch with her every day, calling in by rote. But she still likes to be taken back to her home in order to keep an eye on it. Occasionally she seems lonely, and this is often voiced as feeling unwell. There is little however which a trip to the beach in good company does not put right, returning her quickly to her normal buoyant self. She has also been seen out and about in the local streets, stooped now but still active; she pauses to chat to any children, and, resourcefully contrary to the last, she uses one of her wheelchairs as a walking frame!

…for 'her esteemed contribution to the region'.

## About the Author

Marion Osgood is a retired practice nurse and also pastor's wife. She is now archivist for OMF International (UK), in addition to leading local guided walks, and volunteering with Foodbank.

She has travelled widely, including teaching health issues in China and Romania, and TEFL in Somaliland. It was while visiting in the United Arab Emirates that she met Amal in 1999. (Photo above)

Marion's first book, a biography entitled *"Whatever happened to Kathy Keay?"* was published in 2010. She is currently researching and writing her third book, another biography, about Jennie Hudson Taylor.

For relaxation she and her husband Hugh enjoy country and London walks. They live in Bromley, Kent, and have three grown-up children.

For more information, including how to obtain further copies of her books, please visit www.marionosgood.com

Amal with author (and husband) in 2017

# Bibliography

Awar, Jarrar Nada, *An Unsafe Haven*, London, The Borough Press, 2016

Bell, Gertrude, *The Desert and the Sown*, London, W Heinemann, 1907

Dalrymple, William, *From the Holy Mountain*, London, Flamingo, 1998

David, Anthony, *An Improbable Friendship*, London, Simon & Schuster, 2015

Dyck, Gertrude, *The Oasis*, Dubai, Motivate Publishing, 1995

Hourani, Albert, *A History of the Arab Peoples*, London, Faber & Faber, 1991

Karmi, Ghada, *In Search of Fatima*, London, Verso, 2002

Kay, Shirley, *Land of the Emirates*, Dubai, Motivate Publishing, 1987

McHugo, John, *Syria: From Great War to Civil War*, London, Saqi Books 2014

Meroff, Deborah, *Under their very Eyes*, Oxford, Monarch, 2016

Morton, H V, *In the Steps of St Paul*, London, Rich & Cowan, 1936

Scott, Frances, *Dare and Persevere (the story of the Lebanon Evangelical Mission)*, London, LEM, 1960

Thompson, Andrew, *Christianity in the UAE*, Dubai, Motivate Publishing, 2011

Young, Joann, *"A Tent of His Own"*, Oxford, Bound Biographies, 2016